Closely Watched Shadows

A Profile of the Hunter and the Hunted

Ronald Turco, M.D.

 BookPartners, Inc.
Wilsonville, Oregon

BookPartners, Inc.
P.O. Box 922
Wilsonville, Oregon 97070

For Joanne always

Acknowledgements

We are sculpted by our early experiences in life. Later, people and events change our personal history: the story that each of us has. I thank my parents, Antonetta and Luigi and my sisters and brothers; Millie, Lizzy, Al, Louie, Jim, Frank, John and Sal. They did their best to teach me *the way*.

A big thank you to Ursula Bacon for helping me keep my foot (elbow?) out of my mouth and to Thorn Bacon, my editor, whose equanimity balanced my Italian temperament in times of disagreement. The staff at BookPartners has been wonderful in their exactitude and, most importantly, their cheerfulness and support in this venture.

My friend, Victor Calzaretta, as always, has been "right there." His personal experience in many of life's theaters provided detailed and cogent suggestions for change in the manuscript. To Chuck Taylor I say "thumbs up" to our past and future adventures. Patty and Dave Bishop; thank you for being friends in adversity — nonjudgmental and understanding. High praises to Louie who sat patiently without complaint during the many days of writing this book.

My thanks and admiration to Joanne whose 34 years of encouragement kept the meaning in the action.

Most importantly, I thank the many police officers who have shared their lives with me, both on and off duty. Your friendships have shaped my adult life. I am convinced that your sensitivity, dedication and psychological resilience surpasses mine. I know that you work for God.

Ronald Turco
BPST #19568

Table of Contents

Prologue

The Zen disciple sits for long hours silent and motionless, with his eyes closed.... This is not the nothingness or the emptiness of the West. It is rather the reverse, a universe of the spirit in which everything communicates freely with everything, transcending bounds, limitless.... And the emphasis is less upon reason and argument than upon intuition, immediate feeling. Enlightenment comes not from teaching but through the eye awakened inwardly.

Yasunari Kawabata

It was a warm Spring afternoon and the walk to Kinkaju-Ji temple from the environs of Kyoto was extensive, but on this particular day effortless. Having visited and observed Buddhist ceremonies at the Meji Shrine earlier, I found myself predisposed to an experience that was to become hauntingly evocative of an earlier time, an earlier life, an earlier experience. The closer I came to the Temple, the more people there were and I came to notice school children; they too seemed directed and drawn to the Temple in an apparent state of total bliss. Needless to say, they were like school children anywhere in the world laughing and jostling one another and there were more than a few curious stares at the Caucasian in their midst. The climb to the Temple consisted of traversing through heavy vegetation and tall trees. The entire experience was conducive of a sense of being *one* with the world. A perfect blending of God and nature. Soon I found myself surrounded by large groups of children, hundreds if not thousands, or so it seemed to me, and this only added to the euphoria that I began to experience. By the time I had walked through the Temple, my head was swimming. It was as if I was floating through the clouds and I had a desire to stay there long through the night and into the following day. I found myself ensconced in a sea of children. I became one of them.

How could I have foreseen then, participating as I was in that large group of laughing children, the horror that would come to visit me involving other children half a world away?

Introduction

— · —— · —— · —— · —— · —— · —— · —— · —— · —— · —— · ——

During midlife, contemporary events such as the natural aging process, illness and loss rekindle earlier unresolved issues *as well as* unfulfilled dreams and fantasies. It is a time of change and maturation. Sometimes, as a result of unconscious processes at work, therapeutic intervention is necessary. This book is about all that and a bunch of good guys — ordinary heroes — a real bad guy, romance and Oregon. It's about dedication and hope, the impermanence of life and the interdependency of all living things. Most importantly, it's about what William Faulkner would say: "… man must, does and will prevail."

Passing Shadow

A dark shadow passes across my face;
I am frightened and cry.
Holding your hand helps;
Being a part of you fulfills me.
I write this in a dream;
The bright sun on the snow
Gives me perspective,
The quietness of it all
A sense of wholeness.
We are part of the same world.
Ronald Turco, 1986

Chapter 1

Decayed Angels

———·———·———·———·———·———·———·———·———·———·———·———

All who knew you among the peoples are aston-
ished at you; you have become a horror, and shall
be no more forever.
                    Ezekiel 28:19

The telephone call from the Portland Police Bureau
did not seem out of the ordinary. For years I had been
working with police officers on investigations and, in the
Fall of 1989, I anticipated such "routine" calls for assistance
in my role, not as a psychiatrist, but as a sworn police
officer. The town of Newberg, Oregon, infrequent home of
the late President Calvin Coolidge, about 45 minutes from
Portland, was operational base for me. Other police departments asked for my help — under the interdepartmental
cooperation rule — and I was "loaned out" to assist on cases
throughout the Northwest. I led, and still lead, a double life
— psychiatrist and police officer. This particular call from
C.W. Jensen of the Portland police initiated a series of

events that would change my life, and his, permanently. He and I were to develop a bond that would lead to an odyssey of obsession and horror, but the story began long before the telephone call.

David G. Bishop is a tall, large, robust and, at times, red-faced man. It's been said that his ego is bigger than his frame and some will tell you the "G" in his name stands for God. Be that as it may, he is big-hearted and he is known as a police officers' police officer. He is respected and mostly loved by the men he commands, envied by his peers and feared by his enemies — criminal and political. It is not beyond reasonable judgment to describe him as a tough, innovative police officer with a moral perspective that stems from a deep religious faith — that which I call the "inner light." This is the guiding principle necessary for an officer if he is going to survive his career and keep his sanity intact. You might say that Bishop has an inner faith that good eventually triumphs over evil. Our relationship was not without ambivalence. At times we feuded for months over issues of moral principle.

Once, David kept me waiting outside a courtroom where I was to testify. He could have managed events in a manner that did not irritate me, since I had patients to see in the afternoon. Finally, when he came into the hallway at 12 P.M. I went into a rage, threw a tantrum, and left. About thirty minutes later, when I was back at my office desk, my attorney telephoned and said I was needed as a witness in the afternoon. With tongue in cheek, he said that he and Bishop had considered the idea of beating the hell out of me or bribing me with a case of wine if I went back to court. Of course, I was over my anger by this time, and I made the appearance on schedule.

Some of our disagreements were about people we both knew, especially about their trustworthiness. The differences between David and I continue, and when I tell him that he lacks insight into human nature and is too willing to overlook the faults of friends, he tells me I'm too moody. His own flamboyant style is obvious at police meetings when he grabs me with both arms and plants a kiss on my cheeks. No officer has ever questioned us about this ritual.

What most people who have adopted a skewed view of cops as a result of the fictional portrayal of policemen on TV (hardboiled insensitive men who shoot first and ask questions later) fail to realize is that cops are often victims of the violence in which they participate. One example of the organized effort to provide a healing atmosphere for policemen and policewomen is the Loyola Retreat House. Much time is spent by the attendees in silent prayer and meditation. Conversation occurs at meals and there is an evening of emotional disclosure and sharing of experiences. This is usually a very intense time with tears flowing freely as "tough" officers recount their traumas, problems and preoccupations. After silent prayer and reflection, the men often discuss the need to live for something beyond themselves as well as recognizing the resentments they are prone to carry through life. They learn that such emotional baggage represents obstacles to intimacy with their own families and friends. Deep resentment about "bad guys" — strangers — with whom they come in contact on the job blocks their ability to love.

I recall one particularly enjoyable session when a Jesuit priest we had invited to lead started a game of looking for God. This began with opening cupboards, desk drawers and closets to see if God was around. Our laughter turned serious when the search for God was directed inside ourselves. The retreat ended with a communion ceremony I shared with my brothers. My own religious path is closest to Tibetan Buddhism and encompasses yoga, meditation and experiencing the natural world. The philosophy of one of America's top detectives, Vernon Geberth, one of the most highly decorated police officers in the New York police department, is encompassed in the phrase: "We work for God." Geberth was commander of the Bronx homicide unit and is the author of *Practical Homicide Investigation,* the basic textbook for all investigators. He taught me that homicide investigators are the voice of the dead and are the living representatives of the families of the deceased.

I learned of one officer who, although dying of cancer, insisted on directing a homicide investigation because the victim had been a young child who was assaulted and killed while she was out riding her bicycle. The officer continued to work grimly from his deathbed, and after he died, as a result of his investigation, a suspect was apprehended, found guilty of serial murder and sentenced to life imprisonment. The officer completed a religious journey. What better memorial to a life devoted to service, justice and love?

I came to admire people like Terrence J. Mangan, chief of police of the Spokane Police Department. A former Catholic priest, Terry is famous for trading his clerical collar for a badge in 1970. As a defender of the faith, Terry was always at the forefront of life. He joined the Oratorians, a Catholic order of intellectuals involved in the activist position of advancing changes promoted by Pope John XXIII. He was active in social causes, earned a master's degree in theology and was finally ordained. Terry worked as a reserve police officer in Seaside, California and eventually left the priesthood for a career in law enforcement. He became chief of the Lakewood Police Department outside Los Angeles, and in 1976 became chief in Bellingham, Washington. This led to his investigation of a murder that culminated in the arrest of Kenneth Bianchi, a serial killer — the Hillside Strangler. About ten years later, Mangan became chief of the Spokane Police Department. He continues his interest in reading the New Testament in Greek, Latin, Hebrew, French and German. He considers himself an expert in the adventures of Sherlock Holmes. As Terry Mangan demonstrates, police officers do not fit a stereotype. Fictional accounts and technical studies of police officers describe their unusual camaraderie and sense of righteous indignation when justice is not served for the victims. This sense of bonding and purpose is important, especially in the face of public demands and legal procrastination.

My career in psychiatry in Portland began in 1973, and it was natural to begin work with police officers as an extension of my work with the U.S. Air Force Criminal Investigative Division (CID) and Air Force Intelligence. The military work was both active and academic, and, therefore, very exciting, stimulating and unusual compared to civilian life. In Portland, the work with police officers was somewhat more mundane, involving crisis intervention with officers following traumatic incidents, marriage counseling and teaching stress-reduction techniques. Pre-employment police evaluations brought me into contact with more than 25,000 police candidates. During one of the "sensitivity" sessions at my home, I first met David G. Bishop, then a captain with the Beaverton Police Department, at that time a relatively small agency just outside the Portland metropolitan area. This chance meeting resulted in a major modification of my professional career. The group sessions had their share of humor, with Bishop sitting in my chair, before I had a chance to sit down, to test my reaction. Joanne, my wife, prepared cookies, pastries and coffee for these meetings. After the series of group sessions ended, David and I had some infrequent contact, usually about a troubled officer. My life was going along smoothly and, in addition to a thriving private practice, I received an appointment as medical director of a small psychiatric hospital close by Portland.

On Valentine's Day, 1981, Captain David Bishop was at the altar of St. Ignatius Church taking Holy Communion, surrounded by men whose fate I would later share in a joint quest, and with whom I would bond. Growing up as I did in a family of eight men is conducive to bonding in this way. As he stepped down from the altar and into his pew, David was passed a note regarding an urgent call from dispatch. A seasoned detective knows what's urgent and what isn't. One glance at the note was enough for Bishop to end his contemplation of God and destiny. He thought of his own confession the night before Communion and how good he had felt cleansing himself before God. That good feeling now changed, because Bishop knew something about the chain of events that would soon unfold. He motioned to his men. They solemnly went to their small cell-like rooms where they had stored their police gear, packed quickly and, once outside, donned their weapons. A young woman had been found dead in her home. A short time later, I received a call asking me to assist in the investigation.

This beautiful, popular, young woman, who lived not far from my own home, had been sexually assaulted and shot in the temple on each side of her head. She had been descending a staircase — nude. Bishop wanted a psycho-logical profile to assist in the investigation. Such a profile was a relatively new and unused technique in law enforcement. Arriving at the scene was, in itself, traumatic for me. On a pretty, sunshiny day, I stepped into a comfortable home occupied by a dead woman. During the search of her belongings along with the forensic team, I remained in a state of suspended belief. I told myself this was no movie set, but I wanted it to be one. Just a few hours before, the victim had been alive in the flesh with family, friends, hopes and dreams. The photographs we went through depicted people she knew as well as her interests. Greeting cards told of her affections. Even the dirty clothes in the hamper reflected a life — a life now gone.

The body was that of Julie Ann Reitz, who, it was later learned, had been one of Randall Woodfield's admirers. It was Randall Woodfield, the award-winning student and star athlete, who was finally identified and convicted for several sex-killings, including Julie Ann Reitz. He was the man who had been drafted to play football by the Green Bay Packers, picked by *Playgirl* as a centerfold candidate. As an attractive male working in swinging West Coast bars, he chose among many willing sexual prospects. But Woodfield wanted more than ordinary sex. As Julie's body clearly indicated, she had been raped prior to being shot to death. It was the *True Crime* writer, Ann Rule who described Julie in her book, *The I-5 Killer,* and the scene we found when we entered her apartment:

"Julie, who still lived with her mother and a female roommate in a plush duplex on S. E. Cherryhill Drive in Beaverton, had celebrated her eighteenth birthday only two days before. She had had plans to attend several Valentine's Day parties on Saturday night, although she wasn't going with a date. Both her mother and her roommate were also away until the early hours of Sunday morning.

"When her mother returned home, she found all the lights blazing, and then she saw, on the stairway of the town house, Julie's slender, naked body. Thinking at first that the girl might have fainted, or even passed out after drinking more than she could handle, her mother rushed to help her up. But up close she could see that Julie's long light brown hair was stained mahogany with her own blood. She thought that Julie must have struck her head on the newel post and been knocked unconscious. But Julie did not respond to any stimuli, and her mother dialed frantically for help.

"Ambulance attendants saw almost at once that Julie Reitz hadn't fallen; she had been shot — a near-contact wound to the head — and she was dead. The body was left on the stairway, and Beaverton police were called. Uniformed patrolmen verified that this, indeed, was a homicide, and cordoned off the crime scene to await detectives.

"Captain Dave Bishop and Detective Neal Loper took charge of the case.

"There were no signs of struggle. It looked as if Julie had been running down the stairs toward the front door when she was cut down by bullets. Likely her killer had been just behind her, and he — or she — had stopped the victim from flinging open the door to run for help.

"Julie's mother and roommate said that the door to their home was always locked and that Julie would not have let a stranger in, particularly not late at night. That meant, surely, that her murderer was someone she had known and trusted. And if she'd known her attacker, he might well have felt killing her was the only way to keep his identity secret."

As it turned out, our surmise was correct. Randall Woodfield was a clever monster who lusted after beautiful women whom he could punish with total domination and unspeakable degradation. He cruised I-5 the interstate highway through California, Oregon and Washington until the list of his victims grew to a total of at least 44.

On the surface he appeared too handsome and appealing to have committed such atrocious crimes — ugly acts of murder that filled every woman within his striking range with fear and horror.

Work on this case involved nights and weekends and occasional days off so I could continue with my private practice and earn a living. The police work brought no income nor have I ever asked for any payment for my police investigative work. In the course of the investigation, I became acquainted with dozens of police officers throughout the state who were assisting in linking this particular murder to others with a similar "m. o." We postulated it was likely that the victim had known her killer and our work focused on her friends, acquaintances and people she had last been seen with. During this investigation I learned something about the techniques of interrogation (as opposed to interviewing) including "good guy-bad guy" scenarios and how to "lean" on people. We studied techniques of crime scene examination, the significance of blood splatter, evidence collection and related forensic techniques.

I was not then familiar with Geberth's book on homicide investigation, but that was soon to come. The blood splatter evidence was interpreted by Rod Englert, a county detective and an international expert in this study, who was loaned to other police departments in time of need. In years to come, we would work together again and again. Hampered by a limited departmental budget, we sometimes paid expenses out of our own pocket. We dined on cheeseburgers and coffee.

As a result of my new associations, my life was changing. I began to develop a close sense of camaraderie that is common among police officers and soldiers — those who sometimes have an "us against them" perspective and who rely on one another to stay alive in times of danger. My acceptance in this group was unquestioned, possibly because of the prior work we had done together.

The investigation of the murdered, nude woman was headquartered in a small prefabricated building adjacent to the department proper. The walls were covered with large poster papers outlining the chronology of evidence collection, other similar crimes in the geographic area, ongoing investigations throughout the West, and names and addresses of suspects. Where possible, we listed phone numbers, and most importantly, license plates. This was the kind of scene I was to see over and over again in the next fifteen years. Much of our work involved brainstorming together, reviewing crime scene forensic reports and interrogating potential suspects. We tried to make sense of the data, but interviewing "potentials" was problematic because of the legal restrictions protecting privacy. Many of the people we talked to were still living with their parents, who objected to interrogation of their "children."

We pushed matters as much as we could and were, at times, threatened with legal action. The data we collected were shared with other departments and a pattern began to develop in association with similar homicides in Oregon and California. The murders appeared to follow the Interstate 5 highway. No one wanted to say for sure that we were investigating a serial killer. A task force, including other agencies, was set up to review a series of killings and the pattern soon became unmistakable. We were dealing with a ruthless serial killer. He was going strong and we had no direct clues to his identity. He would go on killing unless we could find him. Dave Bishop became obsessed with this investigation. He bore the brunt of the emotional impact. Police stress was a concept that was just beginning to become recognized at that time. Knowing about this concept didn't help David. Some of the joking and teasing in the group helped ease tension but looking at photographs and examining crime scenes day after day took its toll.

I lost my appetite and some weight. David was touchy — very touchy. Eventually, we collected our thoughts if not our feelings. Bravado and false humor notwithstanding, the pieces began to fit together. Bishop, with his wife, Patty, my wife, Joanne, and I began meeting at our home. On March 15, 1981, Joanne prepared an Italian dinner and, around the dinner table, as strange as it may seem and as gruesome as it may be, we developed a psychological profile of the killer.

On March 20, I began a series of meetings with Detective Englert to fine tune our findings. What fit and what didn't? These meetings continued until April 24. Before my eyes and my soul, the largest criminal investigation in the State of Oregon was in progress, and progressing we were. At that time, little was known about the physical or personal characteristics of serial killers. I tried to formulate various hypothetical constructs but they were not necessarily practical in the investigative sense. Demographic facts were not yet available, and it was to be years later that Pierce Brooks of the Los Angeles Police Department would develop material leading to a Violent Criminal Apprehension Program (VCAP). Years would pass before I would have an opportunity to talk to this legend of a man.

But this was 1981. Once we established links among several murders in Oregon and Washington, we approached the investigation as that of a serial killer. With no precedents to guide me, I fell back on psychological profiles which had been done of political figures and artists. I tried to formulate psychodynamics, that is, motivation and, ultimately, direction. Could we predict what this monster would do next? He seemed to have a penchant for shooting people in the face or head. Of what possible significance could this be? Serial killers are psychologically primitive. Their psychological development is characterized by infantile defense mechanisms and reactions. I was familiar with the work of a psychotherapist by the name of Melanie Klein, who studied primitive reactions and formulated hypothetical constructs about behavior based on early infant experiences, especially with the mother figure. Serial killers act on the fantasies that infants may have, in a much different form, of course. These complicated psychodynamics suspend judgment and morality, and focus on theory and behavior. Serial killers deal with an intense rage, transferred from the mother figure to other women and sometimes men. Even when torturing their victims, they perpetuate the rage and tension through perverted "pleasure" techniques such as slow strangulation, drinking the blood of victims or otherwise devouring them. The ultimate behavior is debasement of the victim and ultimate total destruction — murder. The killers make their victims less human.

All people have psychological techniques for the relief of tension, the protection of the ego from shame or embarrassment, or to deal with fear — internal or external. Serial killers have not developed beyond the stage of "splitting," a mechanism that occurs during the first year of life. It is as if the child is trying to psychologically "split off" good and bad parts of himself and his mother. If this process is accentuated and persists, it becomes highly abnormal. In a flawed adult, good and bad are polarized. In the case of a serial killer, he kills the "all bad" woman, which may be why prostitutes are a frequent target of such killers. He finds them easy to denigrate and dehumanize. They may represent fantasies he has had, either consciously or unconsciously, about his mother. These women are also exposed and very vulnerable.

Using the theoretical "splitting" guideline in the case of the I-5 killer, as he was now known, we hypothesized that he would likely make a telephone call from the scene of his murder victims. Based on the theory of splitting he would kill the "bad mother" and call the "good mother." This acting out was beyond his conscious awareness.

We were aided in our search for the killer by an m. o. that was presented in a conference of police officers in Roseburg, Oregon. Officer Dave Kominek made the description:

"The subject hits various businesses in the evening hours, normally between 5:00 P.M. and 11:00 P.M., with emphasis on the early evening hours. He goes in when there is a lull in business. We believe he is armed with a .32 caliber silver revolver. In most instances, he ties or tapes his victims — with hands crossed behind their backs and ankles crossed. He usually picks businesses with young women on duty, and often with two young women. He has them disrobe, but he only unzips his trousers. He forces victims to masturbate him or to perform oral sodomy. With older females he usually only fondles. He invariably takes his victims to the back of the building where they cannot be seen from the street. He sometimes removes the telephone receiver to prevent victims from calling for help."

Kominek wrote the following description on a blackboard:

"Tape on nose.

"Green jacket or windbreaker-type jacket.

"Hood or ski cap.

"Fake beard.

"Gloves — ski, sporting, driving.

"No odors detected.

"Soft-spoken, rarely uses profanity.

"Macho — considers his penis is large, and brags about it.

"When he leaves, orders victims to count to 100 or 500.

"Vehicle thought to be left several blocks away.

"White male — 25 to 28.

"5'11" to 6'1", medium build.

"Dark hair, possibly curly.

"Dark eyes — 'sad eyes' or 'tired eyes.'

"Good-looking. Possible acne scarring.

"Weapons: .32 caliber, 6-shot revolver, nickel- or chrome-plated. Smith & Wesson model 60 stainless-steel .38 special, 5-shot with a 3" barrel, wood grips.

"Vehicle: Volkswagen Bug?"

There was also a tentative psychological profile to which I contributed:

"Subject is a male Caucasian, possibly recently divorced or separated from girlfriend. Released within the last year from some type of institution. Has a very macho image of himself. Is the type to drive a four-wheel-drive or sports-type car. Uses false beards as a possible macho symbol. The Band-Aid is simply to hide behind. This man is probably the type who would be considered a very nice person by the people next door. Primary motivation is sexually related. Subject is a loner and possibly has latent homosexual tendencies."

"Our man has herpes," Officer Kominek continued. "Several of his victims have contracted the disease after being sexually abused. As far as we know, he has never attempted normal intercourse, his fetish is oral or anal sodomy. I don't have to tell you how frustrating this investigation is. We know what he looks like, we know his patterns, and we even know where he hits — but he's playing cat and mouse with us. When we're looking in Oregon, he's in Washington or California. He may act like a monster, but he looks like the guy next door. There are probably a lot of people who know him well, who think he's a great guy — people who are going to be struck dumb when we catch him. He's as dangerous as any subject most of us will ever encounter, and he's stepping up his attacks. He's killed at least three times, he's attacked children, and he's attacked women. He's in some kind of sexual frenzy. Let's go get him."

Captain Bishop traced a lead to a man named Randall Woodfield living with a female roommate in Eugene, Oregon. Eugene is a university town known for its sports orientation. The University of Oregon boasts one of the finest journalism schools in the country, and the community achieved recognition in the movie *Personal Best.*

When Bishop rang the doorbell of the young woman who had been rooming with Woodfield, she freely answered questions and a lengthy conversation began. The detective asked if he could see some of the latest telephone bills and the request was granted. A pattern unfolded before his eyes. There, in black and white, was evidence of telephone calls made from different places in Oregon and charged to Woodfield's home phone. It was virtually a map of I-5! This was a major piece of evidence linking Woodfield to the series of murders along the I-5 corridor. A search warrant produced other materials — pubic hairs from the bed sheets and a spent cartridge that was discovered in an old gym bag.

Also, Woodfield owned a gold Volkswagen, exactly the same kind of car seen at crime scenes by witnesses.

My telephone rang at 3 A.M. My answering service, no doubt. A patient in trouble, I thought.

"Hello … Ron?… Hello!….this is David." Captain Bishop invited me to join him and the arresting officers going to get Woodfield. My reward.

I declined because of a heavy caseload the following day — besides, my work was over on this case. As events unfolded during the following weeks, we came to believe that Woodfield had committed at least 42 murders in at least three states. Chris Van Dyke, the son of actor Dick Van Dyke, was appointed the prosecuting attorney. This was his first murder case and it was going to be rough. However, a victim, although shot in the face, had lived! The defense counsel found a mercenary psychologist, who testified that the victim couldn't possibly have made an identification. The jury didn't believe him. The evidence was substantial and, despite a good defense team, Woodfield was convicted of murder and sentenced to life imprisonment.

Ann Rule, the crime writer, called me about this case seeking an interview because she was going to write a book about it. I declined to talk to her about it. The horror had been enough for me. I had heard as much as I could bear and I wanted to forget it. She produced an excellent book and years later over lunch, we reminisced about Woodfield and the trail of horror he produced. Bishop collapsed with serious ulcer disease and I went on with my medical practice. I hoped the nightmare would take a back seat in my mind.

It was to be fifteen years later, in collaboration with Vernon J. Geberth, former homicide commander of the New York Police Department, that he and I wrote a paper, based to a certain extent on Woodfield, and of course, on other serial murderers, which described an "organized serial killer." The organized serial killer was originally an FBI concept, although I developed the idea in 1968 when I worked on a series of San Francisco homicides. Woodfield certainly fit the pattern. An excerpt from the forensic literature noted the following:

"The organized offender is usually above average in intelligence. He is methodical and cunning. His crime is well thought out and carefully planned. He is likely to own a car which is in good condition. The crime is usually committed away from his area of residence or work. He is mobile and travels many more miles than the average person. Fantasy and ritual are important to the organized type offender. He selects a victim, whom he considers the 'right type,' someone he can control (either through manipulation or strength), usually a stranger. Most of his victims will share specific traits. He is considered socially adept. He uses his verbal skills to manipulate his victims and gain control over them until he has them within his 'comfort zone.'

"The organized killer is fully cognizant of the criminality of his act and takes pride in his ability to thwart the police investigation. He will often times take a 'souvenir' from his victim that may be used to relive the event or augment the fantasy surrounding the killing. For the organized offender, the souvenir constitutes a trophy. He is excited by the cruelty of the act and may engage in torturing the victim. Sexual control of the victim plays an important part in this scenario.

"The organized offender usually brings his own weapon to the crime scene and avoids leaving evidence behind. He is familiar with police procedures. He will follow the news reports and focus on police statements in an attempt to judge the extent of the investigation. The body is often removed from the crime scene. He may do this to taunt the police by leaving the corpse in plain public view, or to prevent its discovery by transporting it to a location where it will be well hidden."

It was Ann Rule who, I believe, made the definitive, concluding statement on Randy Woodfield, when she described in her book the effect the killer had on a young television reporter:

"One quote about Randy comes back at odd times, late at night, or on a winter Sunday evening in the rain. Dana Middleton, now co-host of her own ABC talk show in Seattle, was a young television reporter in Shasta County in 1981. She covered the murders of Donna Eckard and Janell Jarvis; she pored over police reports on similar cases in the Northwest. And Dana Middleton found herself, finally, in the same room with Woodfield. He was surrounded by detectives, but even so....

"She controls an involuntary shiver as she recalls that night: 'The first time I ever saw him, I noticed he was quite good-looking. But then he turned around and looked at me and I saw his eyes. They were flat. Dead eyes. Shark's eyes. It was exactly like looking into a shark's eyes. There was no emotion there at all, no compassion, just emptiness. I've never seen eyes like that in a human being, never before and never since.'"

Chapter 2

Breaking Cadence

--- -- --- --- --- -- --- -- --- -- --- -- --- -- --- -- ---

A man's fate is his character.
Heraclitus, 500 BC

I learned psychology as a child the easy way. At the dinner table. My father was an Italian immigrant who hated Hitler and loved Roosevelt. It wasn't that simple, of course, but his emotional involvement with politics — and our family — set an example for my life. No demonstration of sterile intellectual exercise on his part, to be sure, for the dinner plates would bounce as he pounded the table to emphasize a point. He was a factory worker caught up in the love and beauty of America and its opportunities for his children. Little could I know that my intense involvement in life's relationships and work would be shaped by the intensity of family loyalties and the love and hate that's generated in the family romance. As an adult psychoanalyst, I learned that Freud taught that we love our enemies and hate even our friends.

My mother, Antoinetta, always the lady, silently acquiesced to Pop's customary behavior. Mom was strikingly beautiful in her youth and she radiated love and tolerance in her maturity. A true angel. What little patience and tolerance I have comes from her teaching, both by work and example. I still remember her giving me advice while tying my shoes in the morning. Shoe tying was always one of my shortcomings and foreshadowed a lack of mechanical perspective still evident.

World War II brought many memories and, at its conclusion, relatives came home with stories and presents from faraway places. I was fascinated by the experiences the men had in Japan, especially since the wartime propaganda did not fit the descriptions I heard of beauty, gentleness and respect — the qualities I admire about the Japanese people. I believe these stories influenced my later passion for contemporary Japanese literature and our family penchant for Japanese exchange students. Finally, I recall my mother in the kitchen one day, characteristically crying profusely and trying to cook at the same time. President Roosevelt had died.

My brothers and sisters were always full of life — competitiveness in our family was a virtue that still is regarded as constructive. Even as illness and death takes its toll of the members, we do not have the pettiness and jealousies I find in many of my patients' families.

Growing up in Philadelphia in the forties and fifties afforded a carefree life to children. Even the war brought people together. The inner city walk to school and games in the street brought no fear to parents concerning the safety of their children. The idea of our modern-day monsters — the pedophiles (one of whom many years later was to draw me into the dark side) — was not even a thought on a faint horizon. My friends and I grew up playing "scoopball" during weekdays after school and "paper football" on weekends. The former consisted of cutting a rubber ball in half and using a broom handle for a bat. The ball was hit toward the house across the street. If it struck the second floor level the score was a double, the third floor a triple and over the roof a homer. Occasionally, we hit a window, but not often. Paper football consisted of rolling up a newspaper the size of a pop can, tying it with cord and going at it. There were also "sword fights" using sticks made from the corner grocer's vegetable boxes. Charlie the fruit man, who was also in the numbers racket, saved the boxes for us and Tony the grocer let us know when the next shipment of wooden vegetable boxes would arrive. Even "crazy Tony" and "crazy James," our neighborhood oddballs, did not have the aura of disease and danger of some of today's schizophrenics. They were accepted as part of life and fed and cared for by neighbors. The War brought everyone together and my family was the center of neighborhood respect and held in high regard.

Perhaps it's no coincidence, considering my later interest in law enforcement, that my best childhood friends had fathers who were police officers. Tommy, who lived across the street, had a father who was a detective in the Philadelphia Police Department — the so called "Red Devils" from the "Round." This title referred to the red police cars they drove and the round, solid granite structure of the police headquarters. Licking ice cones and walking back from the library, a weekly ritual, Tommy and I never dreamed that he would respond to the uncertain trumpet of Vietnam and I would go on to become a physician who would later develop a specialty as a forensic psychiatrist with professional standing as a volunteer policeman.

Why am I relating stories of my childhood? I think the answer is that the warmness and closeness of my family gave me an enduring sense of security that bolstered me and strengthened my identity so that years later when the monsters came to visit me, knocking on the door to my dreams, I had matured into a man who could look on evil and understand its power without being intimidated by its shadow.

Stories are our personal myths, and as such, define our aspirations, fantasies, hopes and fears. I often ask my patients to tell me about some of their childhood memories. Like the Navajo storyteller, these are *their* stories. I recall several quite vividly. On one occasion, my mother departed the house with my sister to go shopping and I was left in the care of my brother, Salvy, who was less than sympathetic about the assignment. On this particular occasion, my father finished off a bottle of the "Dago red" he was fond of making, and went to bed.

Salvy decided that he would start a snowball fight with some neighborhood kids. The momentum was astro-nomical and before I knew it, the older guys, Salvy included, were hard at it throwing ice balls from behind an igloo-style fort. I tried my best to keep up but had none of the throwing power of the big kids. Darkness settled on the city streets where the battle took place. My feet became soggy and cold and my hands were freezing. I begged my big brother to take me home, but to no avail. The battle of Thermopylae was intensifying so I decided to walk home. I discovered the only person in the row house we lived in was my father — fast asleep! Unable to get in the door, my pounding, yelling and bell ringing went on for an eternity before he finally pulled me in out of the cold, took me upstairs and put me in his bed in the front room where my parents slept.

Happy to be under the covers and warm, I soon noticed my father was fast asleep. Some time later, there was an awful commotion outside. "Pop, Pop, I think they're looking for me." My father told me to be quiet and go back to sleep. The investigation into the missing child — me — intensified and an APB was put out, extra available police and detectives combed the neighborhood, and Salvy was scared to death. Had he lost the baby of the family? A rescue truck arrived with sirens full blast, prepared for the worst. Finally, an astute detective found a glove I had dropped on the stairway going up to bed and traced my footsteps to my father's bed. The next thing I remember is sitting on the detective's knee in my shorts squinting at the bright lights around me and my laughing, smiling family much relieved! It's difficult to know what impact this experience had on my personality. Perhaps it influenced me regarding the service aspect of police work — the rescue. Most of all, I'm sure it reinforced the sense of love and acceptance so common in large Italian families. For a while I was the center of attention, showered with demonstrations of affection and love.

Glen Miller and Tommy Dorsey always seemed to be a part of our family and I would not have been surprised if they came walking in the door one day since, in my mind, they were no different from my brother's lookalike friends. In my happy world, everyone was family.

An interesting neighborhood character was old man Shenkel, the corner pharmacist. Shenkel was a bachelor who lived in the back room of his pharmacy and had lots of dusty books with pictures of body parts. On rare occasions when I visited, it was tempting to take a peek. Salvy worked for Shenkel and they had a close bond. Salvy was a hard worker and was well thought of. Shenkel relied on him. One day my brother bought a bicycle, after saving his money for months. My father, who never drove a motorcar, didn't approve but Sal (as we now call him) bought it anyway and hid the bicycle in the back of Shenkel's pharmacy. However, he made one mistake, or, as we shrinks say, a Freudian slip, associated with his guilt over disobeying Pop. He left the wrapping paper the bicycle came in down in our basement. My father found it, surmised what had happened and all kinds of Italian hell broke loose! Sal was forced to return it. It wasn't that Pop was against fun. He was afraid Sal, or any one of us, would get hit by a car. In this way he was very protective. In later years, the family joke was "what kind of a kid grows up without a bicycle?"

My brother Al became a school teacher in the inner city and did a great job with wayward youth; Jim was a war hero, having served in Belgium; Frank served on an aircraft carrier during the war; Lou served in the South Pacific with the army; John became a doctor. Lizzy nurtured all of us and still does the majority of the worrying, and Millie followed in my mother's footsteps as angel. She married young and all the neighborhood children knew they could find cookies and baked goods at her home anytime they wanted. There's a lot I could say about this gang but that would be the topic of another book.

But, as it should be, it was my father from whom I learned a philosophical balance, an equanimity that was to serve me later when I dealt with the darkness that can inhabit the human soul.

From my father I learned to love red wine, intense relationships, politics and, indirectly, psychobiography — the psychological study of individuals. My character development incorporated his directness and integrity. I became his boy and spent evenings sitting by his feet next to our coal stove in the basement. The warmth of the relationship and the hot coals permeated my life until, when I was ten years old, Luigi died.

His had been a lingering and painful illness in which I had played a part. Many years later, during my psychiatric training and personal psychoanalysis, I realized the impact of that early loss and its significance in my life. His last request was that I take care of my mother. This made little sense since I was the youngest of a large family and hardly in a position to take care of myself, let alone anybody else. At this point, however, I became a soldier — *un soldato* — a militant follower, worker and leader — roles I continue to the present day. My definition was cast. Heraclitus believed that the soul itself was related to the essence of life and beyond the mere material — men's souls and behavior were connected to the world as a whole and that one survives death. This is a Buddhist conceptualization in its pure form. We all follow the scripts set out for us in early development and, for better or worse, live our lives, make our mistakes, accomplish what we will and then, like shadows, pass on. I have no complaints and long ago reconciled the passing.

The soldier in me continued to characterize my behavior and personal traits — goal directedness, organization, neatness and a frugal, no nonsense approach to life. I had not expected to change nor ever even thought about it. Somewhat tolerant of others who did not meet my "standards," I was also intolerant in a quiet kind of way. This all came to an end when I came face to face with a horror I could not control. It was a horror that gripped my very soul and purpose for living. It wracked my identity and shook the core of my senses. Subtly, gradually, I tripped into an abyss and fell to rock bottom.

Chapter 3

Kidnapped

How art thou fallen from heaven, O Lucifer,
son of the morning!
                    Isaiah 14:12

The psychological profile, in composite, that we developed of Randall Woodfield — a man no one knew was behind the killings — was remarkably accurate and directly predicted his behavior, which led to his arrest. For the time, and the state of the art of forensic investigation, our deductions were remarkable. We were working long before the development of specific data files of murderers and before the full acceptance of psychological techniques by police departments. A similar lack of appreciation persisted concerning information available from students of satanic cult practices. Crimes of the occult, of devil worship, were predictable based on knowledge that was held in suspicion by police investigators. Fortunately, this has changed. David Bishop was open minded enough to foresee the potential application of psychology to law enforcement and gave it status by his recognition of its value. Nonetheless, it was a beginning science, albeit an accurate one when applied to case solving with intelligence and care. In this respect, there was a series of homicides in California in the late 1960s, and the police dubbed the perpetrator the "Zodiac Killer." I was called on to prepare a profile for the Vallejo Sheriff's Office. It was of little help as the killer was never apprehended.

My involvement in the I-5 case led me to an intense interest in police work and the desire to become a sworn police officer on a consistent basis and not just for individual cases. This would be important in managing parts of investigations, sorting through evidence and marking its "chain" as well as gaining the confidence of other officers in various departments. I could not be just another "shrink." After some legal study, firearms training, physical testing, academy classes and a few formalities, I was sworn in as an officer with the Newberg Police Department. My previous teaching experience at the Advanced Police Academy in Portland accelerated my police certification. In Oregon, sworn officers are given a number by the Bureau of Police Standards and Training. I was issued BPST #19568. By this time Captain Bishop had accepted the post as chief of the Newberg Police Department.

My swearing-in ceremony was characterized by Bishop's sense of humor. Just at the point of completing the oath and agreeing to defend the Constitution of the United States and the laws of Oregon, I was given a campaign hat with a wide brim to put on. These hats are similar to the kind worn by state police officers throughout the United States. As I put the hat on, it fell apart! The brim separated from the top and rolled down my face much to the pleasure and laughter of the onlooking officers. Joanne, who was present, didn't at first know what to make of it. The photographs that appeared in the newspaper the following day were kindly edited to show a more dignified pose with my right hand raised — and no hat!

I learned more and more about police procedures and techniques. Eventually, the homicide work extended to arson and kidnapping. I compare my involvement with the police to that of an anthropologist immersing himself in another culture. Working in two professions, which at first glance appeared to be very different, soon proved to be complementary. Not only had my long-standing interest in psychobiography and psychological profiles found a practical application, but the "people" orientation of the police officers themselves was not unlike the perspective of community mental health workers. But the work was always varied and seldom without surprise. We dragged bodies, living and dead, out of dumpsters, which at times was frightening. We responded to domestic quarrels, vandalism, destruction of churches, "routine" traffic stops and ghastly traffic accidents. Acts of compassion and warmth blended with acts of cynicism and callousness. I met heroes, "sleeze balls," and victims who should not have been victims. The work reflected a microcosm of life, only more intense and emotional. My experiences ranged the gamut of human development, from compassion and heroism to the total denigration of human life, brutality and sadism. It is beyond rational belief how the average police officer handles this bombardment of human frailties.

The officers I came into contact with were compassionate, although they often kept this part of themselves hidden. Some officers develop a cynical attitude, especially regarding the criminal justice system. This could be an insidious and very destructive phenomenon, which reached full recognition at about the seventh or eighth year of an officer's career. Rancor toward "the system" can become malignant and permeate the officer's personal life and intimate relationships. These often were relationships frequently already strained due to shift work, "war stories" and unresolved grief and anger that the officer brought home to his family. Typically, these men were officers who hid the ugliness of police life from public view. While the public may focus its interest on a particularly sensational crime, it is never privy to the gory details. To some extent, psychiatrists face a similar problem of "stuffing" violence and some develop a malaise that can lead to suicide.

In selecting police candidates to become officers, I looked for positive early-parental-relationships and accomplishments in the context of team participation. The ability of an officer to follow through with goals, individually chosen or assigned, is also important. A spiritual perspective is important, along with its associated sense of values based on a "higher power." This is the sustenance for adversity and challenge.

I always thought that Jeanne Boylan, the well known police artist, was a good example of a psychologically healthy person. She was involved in the Polly Klaas kidnapping case and the Oklahoma City bombing. Her investigative interviewing combines a cognitive system and psychological techniques for interviewing high trauma victims. She gains access to their subliminal memory — hidden below the surface — by eliciting positive responses in the face of horror, and draws the memory they describe. The police divers searching for bodies following the explosion of Flight 800 serve as another example of compassion and dedication — and emotional stability.

The men and women of the Newberg Police Department were wonderful in every respect. I've always admired their lack of cynicism or judgmental attitude. This has also been a department free of racial prejudice, racial slurs or sexual discrimination. In regard to these issues I never heard a "negative." Each officer was unique. Our dispatch officer was sworn and she also worked as the department photographer. She had been the "Ivory Soap Baby," so familiar to the American public. Obviously photogenic, she gravitated into police work following a friendship with the movie star Angie Dickinson, and she worked on the set when the police stories were filmed. Once I asked her how she managed to tolerate photographing the gruesome homicide scenes and she said she thought of them as movie sets with makeup and props!

The use of detachment and humor, so important for stress reduction, was not lost on me. Once, I planted a filmy, lacy negligee in the ammunition box located in the trunk of my car. I knew the sergeant, a very formal person, would use my car for equipment distribution at firearms practice. Well, as expected, he saw it, turned three shades of red and reported it to the chief who responded with rolls of laughter. On another occasion, during a solemn retreat at Loyola, I walked through the hall in a nightgown. Joanne lent it to me for the humorous interlude. When other officers inquired about this unusual sleeping attire, the guys in my department told them I was simply unusual. They loved every minute of this, especially after I proved I could handle the rough and tumble of police work. I became involved in the routine duties of a police officer, including felony traffic stops, and my fellow officers knew they could rely on me. Most of the time I put in was on weekends and evenings,

although Bishop eventually appointed me hostage negotiator which meant 24-hour on-call. This didn't seem like
much because in a small town it's unlikely to have a hostage
situation. Other departments "borrowed" me for help with a
psychological perspective on investigations — especially
homicides. Gradually, the Oregon State Police asked for my
services and, as a result of these involvements, there were
frequent television interviews for the evening news. Most of
my friends and colleagues assumed I earned a living doing
police work. As my television appearances have become
more frequent in recent years, my friends probably still
believe this. The work was diverse. When the annual
meeting of the IACP — the International Association of
Chiefs of Police — was held in Oregon, I was stationed at
the top of a statue overlooking the convention hall. They
issued us high powered rifles in addition to side arms in the
event of a terrorist disruption. Although there were some
political demonstrations outside the building, especially by
Communist groups, security was tight and the meetings
occurred without disturbance.

One evening in 1984, I received an urgent call from
dispatch. I was needed immediately! There had been a
kidnapping and the officers wanted my assistance but the
dispatcher was unable to tell me what the urgency was. With
little information to go on, I was annoyed and thought of
ignoring the call. Surely, there were plenty of officers to
work on this. Fatigue was taking its toll on me and my
temper was apparent much more often. People began to tell
Joanne that I was touchy.

Of course, it had been "one of those days." Everybody
wanted something and I felt drained. It was well after 7:00
P.M. when I arrived home in the worst possible mood.
Needing some time to relax before dinner, I poured myself

a glass of red wine and went directly to my study. The mail was piled high — mostly bills — but before I had a chance to either open them or take a sip of the wine, the telephone rang.

Dispatch explained that the kidnapping was just a few hours old. I knew from experience, personal and professional, that police wait at least 24 hours before an APB is sent out or a search conducted.

"What's the big deal?" I asked.

Dispatch knew next to nothing about this situation. Apparently the dispatcher was also working on a major fire during this time, dispatching rescue vehicles and fire trucks to an apartment fire. I thought I'd pass on this one. A few minutes went by, and I guess my guilt or sense of responsibility got the best of me. I called the department again. This time Stan, one of our best detectives, answered. As usual, he spoke calmly and I knew the tone of his voice or rate of speed had little to do with the gravity of any situation. People like Stan and Paul, an FBI agent I knew, were the type who respond to difficult situations with apparent casualness, but always competently and with excellent results. Real "pros."

Stan explained that the kidnapping involved a small child taken either by a stepparent or a boyfriend of the mother. The problem was that this individual was high on cocaine and he had eluded police in Portland and fled to Newberg. Now holed up in an old apartment house, he could occasionally be seen in the window with a .357 magnum pistol aimed at the child's head. This vengeful behavior was directed toward the baby's mother. The kidnapping had turned into a hostage situation. This had reached crisis proportions and as the officially designated hostage negotiator, I was expected to arrive on the scene as quickly as possible. This was easier said than done. I briefly spoke to Joanne, who was preparing dinner, donned my bulletproof vest, which I wore under a fatigue shirt, and put on combat boots. Over the vest, I wore a flak jacket from my military days. It had steel-reinforced plates. After strapping on two weapons, an automatic and a revolver, I picked up the kit I keep for such emergencies. It had extra gloves, a helmet, flashlight, handcuffs, a camera and related paraphernalia. I used my blue light on top of the car. This is a magnetic device used by plain-clothes detectives to better maneuver through traffic in emergencies. I hoped the drive would be less than 45 minutes. It was late, but it was also getting dark and I didn't see as well in subdued lighting.

During the drive, I reviewed what information I had been given and what I might say or do at the scene. Joanne had told me to be careful. I didn't consider that she might be worried! She's the type of person who doesn't put prestige or position above quality in a person, but nevertheless, when you're married to a doctor, you don't expect this kind of turmoil.

Thinking about the kidnapping, I remembered a personal event which occurred some months before. Joanne went out to pick up a pizza at a nearby hoagie shop. About three-quarters of an hour passed and no Joanne. An hour went by and I really started to worry. Deciding to investigate this situation myself, I strapped on a shoulder holster with my .45 caliber Sig Sauer and two extra clips of ammunition. Driving through the park that intervened between our home and the pizzeria, I looked at every bush and tree and suspiciously strained my eyes. No Joanne. The man at the pizzeria said that no one with her description had been in. I really started to worry. At home again, there was little

I could do except to call police friends. Dave Bishop said
they wouldn't file a missing persons report until at least 24
hours passed. Joanne had been gone an hour and 45
minutes. This occurrence stood out as an example of the
increasing distrust I had developed regarding events and
people. I was thinking like a police officer.

More than two hours after she left, Joanne arrived
home with the pizza. She had gone to a nearby bookstore to
read while they made the pizza and had become absorbed in
a book. I was both angry and relieved and called the people
I had notified to report the good news. This became a
standing joke with our friends as well as with Joanne, but I
failed to see the humor in it. I did, however, tell her in no
uncertain terms that the next time she was kidnapped while
buying a pizza, I would not respond!

By the time I arrived at the scene of the hostage
situation, inside and outside perimeters had been established. The operation was following the book — just as we
had rehearsed. A few years before, I had given a hostage
negotiation lecture at the police bureau, which led to the
establishment of a master plan for hostage situations.

The hostage taker was seen intermittently with the
child. Although he was confined, he was certainly active.
He was firing randomly and seemed to have plenty of
ammunition. The situation had escalated to the point where
Chief Bishop had had to take over the negotiations. This had
happened before I arrived and was a necessary break in
protocol. Had I been close by, the negotiations would have
proceeded differently.

A hostage taker with a gun is a frightening prospect,
and one on drugs is even more frightening. For some
reason, I worried about getting shot in the head, especially
around the eyes. The squad cars offered some protection but

we had to be very careful not to provoke this guy, whoever he was. Drugs and alcohol make the situation especially unpredictable and are never negotiated or traded during such times. Part of our problem was that the ultimate decision maker, the chief, was handling the negotiations and this is never a good idea. The hostage taker should know that decisions about his requests are made by someone else, which also allows an opportunity to buy time. Time is the negotiator's ally. The most dangerous period during the hostage situation is the initial assault phase and the situation peaks in about ten to twelve hours. At this point, one has a pretty good idea of what is or is not going to happen and also intelligence gathering can provide background information obtained from various sources. Time also helps to reduce the hostage taker's expectations. We work toward making him feel more comfortable to reduce his anxiety, thus minimizing the threat of violence or impulsive reaction. I also like to send in water and food, partly to increase the perpetrator's need to go to the bathroom. This makes him more like the people he is holding and "reduces" him to a human level, like everybody else, and also provides for moments of distraction.

Darkness fell quickly. I was soaking wet with perspiration. The hardware was heavy and tight. Bishop and his team did a good job. Eventually, the baby was rescued and the bad guy came out. Incidentally, we do call them bad guys. Someone handed me the baby, I guess because I'm a doctor. She seemed okay and I was satisfied she was not harmed, although she was wet and soiled. This baby clearly had not been changed or cleaned in some time. At this point I fought back tears. I remembered that once, when I worked the emergency room at a Pennsylvania hospital, a small child who had been hit by a car was handed to me. My left hand cupped his head and the sensation of multiple bone fragments stunned me. That child died.

I took the baby to the chief's office; the child's mother was already in there. She took one look at me, my dirty face, perspiration drenched fatigue shirt with the name Turco clearly visible and said angrily: "Who the hell are you?"

Stunned, I said nothing. The chief intervened on my behalf and said I was one of his men. He explained that I was one of the people who had been up all night trying to rescue her little girl. Before he finished speaking, she grabbed the baby from me and abruptly left the office. That mother has never thanked me or acknowledged any of our roles in this risky rescue attempt. This was not unusual and is a frequent phenomenon with pararescue personnel. The man, the hostage taker, was the ex-spouse of the woman. He was bitterly angry with her. He was later released.

I was leaving the department for the drive home, feeling proud. Bishop said I was one of his men! Before leaving, I made the acquaintance of a Portland police detective who had tracked the perpetrator from Portland to Newberg. He was one of two detectives who had been in pursuit of this man for the better part of the day and a long night. His name escaped me at the time, but he remembered me down to the closest detail.

Arriving home as others were preparing to go about their daily business, I found that Joanne was still asleep. She woke up momentarily and I asked if she had been worried about my safety. She groggily responded that that was the reason she was still asleep. Perhaps this scenario was nothing new. Her father had been a policeman and after retirement pursued a second career in law enforcement.

I showered, dressed and prepared to face a day of patients, each with his own story — his own drama. They would remain unaware of mine. I struggled somewhat to put the night out of my consciousness and to deal with the adrenaline flow. Somehow I still wondered if what I had witnessed and took part in had been real.

Chapter 4

Battlefield of the Spirit

———·——·——·——·——·——·——·——·——·——·——·——·——

His was a battlefield without glory, a battlefield where none could display deeds of valor: It was the front line of the spirit.
Mishima (Patriotism)

Joanne is different. Our friends as well as strangers will agree. Quiet, composed and at times with a penetrating stare, she can put you at ease or make you uneasy. As companions for more than 34 years, we have traveled the shared journey of life. We've taken its knocks and its good parts. Most of all, we're a team. Our relationship is personal, not social and not professional. Most people don't understand the candor we display or the differences we have in personality and style. We are distinctly two different people on the same team. Joanne was with me in the Soviet Union, we toured medical facilities in remote tribal villages in Africa and we watched the Portuguese revolution from the secure post of a high-rise hotel in downtown Lisbon. I am with her.

Joanne has several college degrees, including one in history and Latin American studies of which she is most proud. She is the most in-depth and diverse reader I know, with special interests in international fiction. Our best time together is spent walking in the countryside or reading to one another and comparing ideas and notes from different books. I rarely ever mention work in psychiatry or law enforcement. The time we spend together is much deeper in the philosophical and emotional realms. In the course of my life and work, I've observed a lot of relationships and I doubt if many approach our level of candidness or resoluteness. When faced with a crisis, we move in unison, but when our goals diverge, Joanne holds her turf. This nononsense quality broadcasts resoluteness to everyone around, yet the gentleness with which this is communicated is hauntingly evocative of my mother's persona. Once, in the middle of the night, a man jumped from the rooftop of our house to the outside deck in a burglary attempt. I held him at bay with a semiautomatic and Joanne, without words, left the room and telephoned the police. The unspoken swiftness with which we acted resulted in a positive resolution.

Joanne is no stranger to evil. She knows it exists, having experienced it first hand. Living on an Air Force base near missile silos, we would follow closely the casualty reports from Vietnam, sometimes finding our friends on the list. The silent grief of past losses is never completely resolved.

In 1989, she watched the progression of an evil encompass me to the very foundation of my soul. A friendship, a marriage and a life were gradually being choked off. She doesn't like to rehash the past. I do. As a physician, I think it's therapeutic. As a human being, I have to. I believe we must come to grips with ancient history, that recapitulation leads to redemption. Perhaps God doesn't work in personal ways ... perhaps he does.

I'm no stranger to death. Even before the completion of my medical studies, I worked the big city hospitals where on Friday and Saturday nights we were faced with the aftermath of the "knife and gun clubs." Many patients died in my arms and it was never comforting to pronounce them dead. After medical school, I took an additional year of medicine and surgery and many of my chronically ill patients died. It's truly remarkable how close one becomes to people who are sharing their last moments on earth with you. One individual left me his body after he died. I was sure his was not a suicide, as some believed, and ordered an autopsy. When that proved negative for medical causes of death, I insisted on the cranium being opened. It was not routine to open the head in autopsies in the sixties.

"It's my body and I want the head opened!" I insisted.

This persistence uncovered the cause of death — a large tumor that had gone undetected. This discovery allowed the family of the deceased to recover the insurance payment that otherwise would have been canceled in the case of suicide. Why did this man leave me his body?

In the emergency room, it was not unusual to carry a child directly to the autopsy table. Policemen and doctors will tell you that it's hardest with children. They don't forget the faces and the circumstances. Joanne's father reinforced what I had already discovered: grief, desperation and, at times, fear do compromise your effectiveness. I witnessed acts of valor and dedication. Such a one was embodied in the compassion of Andrew Wyeth, the artist, who visited his close friend, Carl, on a regular basis and never lost touch with his humanity. In another example, one of my patients gradually died as a result of lymphatic cancer. Daily, her close friend came to the hospital to change the bandages of pussy, draining wounds and give her dying friend solace and encouragement. I will never forget these acts of compassion and dedication — ordinary people, ordinary heroes.

I became commissioned in the U. S. Air Force in 1967 as a first lieutenant. I had finished medical school and was commissioned by a very dear friend of mine who went on to become a surgeon. He was in the navy. He read the oath to me and it was a big deal. I had several reasons to join the military that I thought were important. All my family had served in the armed forces and I thought it was about time that I did. And of course, the Vietnam war was on.

Though I was sworn in in 1967, I was able to defer active duty until I finished surgery training. Then, I went on to psychiatry at North Carolina, followed by two years at the University of Oregon. In all, I had three years of psychiatry before I went on active duty in 1970. For a time, my home base was Anchorage, we lived at Elmendorf Air Force Base.

I discovered many ordinary heroes during my tour in the U.S. Air Force. I was involved in military intelligence, training that was invaluable for my career later. Because I believe in the cause of America so deeply, I could embrace military life with gusto, volunteering for everything that came along. I liked the training, the protocol, the combat boots and the camaraderie. At times, I lived in Spartan conditions underground and under the ice at U.S. missile bases in the Arctic. Thriving on the pace and intensity, I traveled and reveled in the decision making and unexpected circumstances.There was a brief experience on a submarine and travel to remote outposts. Gradually, the areas of international terrorism and hostage negotiations became paramount in my study schedule, and in the last year of military service, I excelled in some of the cryptic intricacies of intelligence work. My code name was Maxwell, code sign Quebec Kilo followed by several digits. As a civilian in the late 1970s, I revisited Czechoslovakia and was detained under armed guard. This arrest may have been for administrative reasons but I thought back to my service days and worried. My interrogator who called himself my interviewer provided vodka and I consumed close to a fifth, remaining stone sober.

My trip to the Soviet Union was clandestine in nature and I have never been back to Moscow or Leningrad.

My uniforms were tailor made and my shoes always spit shined. Friends called me "General" and I secretly liked the sobriquet. During childhood, the school nurse also called me General.

There was an incident in the Arctic, which happened about six o'clock one cold November night, that I'll always remember. I was in overheated base housing with Joanne, who had just served a delicious meal of caribou and broccoli. While we were eating spumoni ice-cream, we received an urgent phone call. A troop transport plane carrying about 230 soldiers bound for Vietnam had crashed on takeoff. It was about 30 degrees below zero outside. I dressed in polar clothes and bunny boots, the latter being protective foot gear issued for arctic troops. They made driving difficult and my windshield was obscured by ice even though the car had been "plugged in" to the house for interior heating and engine water circulation. Fortunately the battery hadn't gone dead. I raced onto the runway, breaking some traffic rules, to help with the triage and transport of bodies. The scene was one of controlled pandemonium and my actions didn't help matters any. Before starting the car, I sprayed ether into the carburetor and up the tail pipe, something I learned to do to start the car quickly in sub-zero temperatures. While driving to the crash site on the airfield, the ether exploded. I stopped the car, ran away and let it burn. I don't much like cars anyway.

We carried men soaked in JP4 aircraft fuel to safety and wrapped them in blankets. We treated them at the hospital close by. My friend Igor helped. We lost 47 fine men that night and a little bit of my heart. I wasn't sure, but I thought Igor was crying. We drowned our feelings in humor and, always best at it, Igor put up a sign over the makeshift morgue: "Not a good place to be." Everyone in our unit received an Air Force commendation. I wore it next to the weapons qualification ribbons. The grimness of this forged a bond. Igor also taught me to be a little more patient with my daily schedule and to handle each crisis a little more calmly. He was always testing limits, though, and eventually refused to wear combat boots. I wrote him a medical excuse stating he had a cartilaginous disease that was painful with tight footwear. I guess I admired him because he acted out the things I secretly and unconsciously wanted to do.

One typical day while I was in the service, I sat studying a photograph of Idi Amin. He was a bullish appearing man, rumored to have syphilis and mental illness. He was brutal. Putting the picture down, I sorted through the neatly piled dossiers collected by spies and informants. The data was enough to formulate a profile and anticipating his behavior was easy. Doing something about it was another issue. My developing interest in psychological profiling had been reinforced by my recent trip to the Soviet Union using a civilian address and occupation as cover. I saw first hand the grim realities of the East. This interest in profiling was to have a profound effect on my life and career more than twenty years later. The decision to give up a career in intelligence and settle in Portland was not easy but was based on a number of personal reasons related to lifestyle and geographic opportunities. I still revel in the sense of freedom we Oregonians have, our diversity and our love of the outdoors.

Shortly after moving to Portland, while driving downtown, I spotted Senator Wayne Morse, whose opposition to the Vietnam war was both legendary and clairvoyant. Stopping in the middle of the street, I left the car, ran up to him and said: "Hi, I'm Ron Turco and I just wanted to say hello!" He grabbed my hand in both of his. "How nice of you to stop, Ron ... I'd like you to meet my friend, Senator Mike Mansfield. Why don't you come into the hotel and have coffee with us?" And that was my introduction to Oregon!

It was several years later that I received a telephone message in November, 1989. It said simply: "Detective Jensen. Portland Homicide. About investigation. Please return his call."

I wasn't interested in responding. Call it a funk maybe, but perhaps this was a prelude to disaster. Maybe my armor wasn't as thick as I thought. My analyst might call some of my behavior "narcissistic omnipotence." I was tired, behind schedule and more moody than ever.

Since I rarely watch television or read the local papers, I had no clue as to what violence may have inspired the call. However, the communities of Portland and Vancouver became consumed with the deaths of three children in a two-month period. Community leaders and politicians were demanding police action. Politicians are the first to criticize, followed by lawyers. Hysteria was building; there were no leads in the killings and public relations was going down the tube. Even the real estate agents were demanding something be done. Who wants to live in a community where children are killed? I finally learned that C.W. Jensen, who had been one of the detectives in the Newberg hostage case years before, had submitted my name as an expert who should be included in the task force being formed to find the killer of the children. Jensen wanted me to profile the killer. He wanted to know what kind of a person would kill children. As if I knew!

"Maybe you can do a profile?" he said. "How about meeting with us today?" he asked me by phone.

In retrospect, his call precipitated a series of events in my life that would lead me to desolation and depravity.

C.W. Jensen is a large, tightly muscled man, and he embodies the prototype of a police detective. Good looking, with fine, piercing eyes, he speaks with a steady baritone. Known as "C.W.," this distinguishes him from another officer, Cliff Jensen. C.W. adopted this nickname and liked to be called simply "C.W." I actually did the psychological evaluation of him when he joined the police bureau. He tested well and his square jaw and broad shoulders were impressive. At 22, he made the most arrests in one of Portland's toughest neighborhoods, became a detective in 1985, and has been a rising star ever since. He was the youngest detective in the homicide unit, unpretentious and competent, clear and calm. Once he was asked to be part of the police programs that are filmed "live" for television. His humor about the invitation was so sardonic and infectious that he was called on the carpet for it. He took the reprimand in his stride. Psychiatrists as a whole could take a leaf from C.W. They take themselves too seriously. I hoped that fault was not one of mine, but I readily accepted the assignment to the task force.

About six weeks earlier, on September 4, 1989, the bodies of two young children had been found in a park in Vancouver, Washington, across the Columbia River, a few minutes drive from Portland. On October 24, the police in Portland were alerted to the disappearance of a young child. On November 1, Vancouver police detectives were directed to the nude body of a white, five-year-old male who, it was later learned, was the boy who disappeared from Portland. A hunter was startled when he came upon the boy's body in the marsh near Vancouver Lake.

The multidimensional task force assigned to investigate the murders included C.W. Jensen, Rick Buckner, Dave Trimble, two Vancouver detectives, two nondescript FBI agents and me. We were supposed to locate the perpetrator. The children had been savagely killed and there are few crimes that polarize a community and mobilize law enforce-ment as much as the murder of a child. A task force is formed to get quick action, to supersede interdepartmental and juris-dictional boundaries. In this case, our job was to find a monster, a horror. There were no leads. There were some clues. I knew, as we embarked on the investigation, that the horrors of life we encountered are, in some ways, a projection of our own interior horrors. It may be hard to understand, but our internal conflicts are projected to an opponent but, in truth, we are dealing with ourselves. That is what makes homicide so difficult to face, for the mythological aspect of our lives manifests in times of crisis when the hydra monster lurking in the darkness we dare not probe lifts her coiled, serpent heads and amazes us with the depth of her evil.

I just knew I wanted to solve a puzzle and catch a killer. Perhaps be drawn into a spiritual crusade. The spiritual power for the battle I was to face was given to me long before I became a policeman or a doctor.

My uniform, badge, gun and intellectual skills would be put to the test again, this time for high stakes. I would descend into that frightening underworld — of depravity— and would have to anticipate the monster's moves. There was nothing high blown about my motives, but I knew the investigation would take me into a search for truth of some kind. I thought about Jane Simon and Richard Chessick, two well known psychoanalysts I greatly admired. Both brilliant with broad perspectives on life, they understand the psyche.

It was Chessick who once pondered whether or not man was a genetic failure. Even animals have systems to avoid unnecessary aggression, he observed. Jane Simon wrote of soul death, while Richard Chessick spoke of malignant transformation. Was the monster we sought a person whose soul was blighted by unfathomable darkness? Surely so, I thought. I knew for certain that I had been drawn into a battle of the spirit. My soul was the ransom.

Chapter 5

Paper Tiger

—·—·—·—·—·—·—·—·—·—·—·—·—

Murder though it hath no tongue will speak.
Shakespeare

In the spring of 1984, I found a round-trip ticket to Japan on my desk. It was the typical, unselfish gesture of the kind that came naturally to Joanne.

"Of course you should go!" she said. "You've always wanted to."

Hers was a birthday present I had never asked for but certainly longed for. Contemporary Japanese literary tradition held a fascination for me as did the work of movie director Kurasawa. Of course, I did make the journey five years before the triple homicide that drew me like a drowning person deep into the darkness of a twisted soul. And the memories of my Japanese journey were restorative. When I needed beauty to refresh myself, I thought of the Kinkaku-Ji temple and escaped in reverie the murder of the children.

But events of the investigation were persistent; they forced their way into my consciousness and I talked to Dave Bishop about my emotional state. He understood and did what he could to be helpful. I recalled what a physical wreck he had become after the Woodfield conviction — the I-5 serial killer who was probably responsible for more than 44 murders. He paid a heavy price for that work. His heart, body and soul were worn out. So was his stomach, and he landed in the hospital with ulcer disease so serious that extensive surgery was required. I didn't think I'd have this kind of problem. My manner is not pushy — at least not directly — but I'm the type of person who *gives* ulcers, not gets them. I was not the responsible person in the present investigation. Part of being a psychiatrist includes an extreme sensitivity and ability to empathize with others. This is perhaps more important than technical knowledge. It causes pain — my colleagues call it "people pain." In my life, issues become personal and intense.

As time went on, I became increasingly absorbed in the investigation. Obsessed would be a better word. Putting my work aside, the focus was on the tracking of a killer or killers. I studied everything I had previously read about pedophilia, and searched out new material. After all, I was expected to know the subject, have the details — the magic.

The task force meetings were casual in nature. Lots of coffee. Lots of talk. Mostly, I talked and everyone wrote. Pedophilia was the principal subject and I gave the detectives everything I had learned about the condition. The coffee at these meetings psyched me up. My nerves were shot. The crime scene photographs and autopsy Polaroids were awful. I loved pathology in medical school, but would never have considered entering such a specialty because autopsies bothered me. One of the murdered children, Lee Iseli, had ligature marks around his neck.

"Why?" we asked.

His anus looked irritated. His closed eyes looked angelic. Studying photographs of the two Neer boys, I was suddenly struck by a thought that had been nagging me for some time. I realized they were dressed in clothes I typically wore as a boy when I was their age. I was especially disturbed by the plaid shirt worn by one of the boys, now splattered with blood. It was enough to make a grown man cry. I noted that Lee's wrists were chafed. Restraints? Most likely. Even after the elapse of time, I can still visualize their bodies as clear as day. The marks of abuse, of sexual stigmata, were signposts advertising the depravity of the killer.

This was no case for a psychiatrist to pontificate on in the quiet of the consulting room. This was a raw, brutal murder. The terrible feelings that it evoked in the spectator were all the more horrible because each member of the task force who viewed the evidence in the photos felt strong rage. It was mixed with a sense of overwhelming guilt for being a member of the same human race that could produce the sexual predator who had killed by design, and, as we later discovered, abused more than 80 other children before turning to murder.

My own feelings were complicated. In college, one of my favorite English professors had asked my why I was not considering a career in teaching. My reply was that I wanted to experience the "realness" of life. I wanted to "be" life, not write about it. Well, this was it! The horror of it was expressed for me by Jacqueline Kennedy, who said after her husband was shot, "I want them to see the horror of it." This was her response when someone asked why she hadn't changed her blood-spattered dress on Air Force One before deplaning. There was evidence of horror also on the bodies of the Neer boys — slice marks from a knife. I hesitated to classify them as neat, for the word used in that context seemed blasphemous.

I made a point of advising the task force in my strongest language that the killer, certainly a pedophile, had reached a point of disintegration. I knew the killing would go on. The perpetrator was motivated by a strong sexual compulsion superseding any sense of civilized morality. But it was also true that sexual predators do have a choice and can stop themselves. I did not for a moment believe that our killer would cease his bloodletting. Every sign he had left on the bodies of his victims convinced me that he was dedicated to the powerful urge that drove him.

Sexual predators strangle or use knives. They generally don't use guns. They can easily overpower children, so there is no requirement for firearms. Also, guns are impersonal. I knew that serial killers of adults don't use guns and I personally believed that, because guns are very masculine tools, sexual predators avoid them. Deep down inside, in the unconscious of these perpetrators, is the absence of a masculine orientation. They are not psychologically intact. They do not choose a weapon of direct aggressive expression. The theory is less important than the results though. In the case of the three slain boys, the positioning of the bodies and examination of clothing strongly suggested the killer's sexual intent. In fact, the autopsy of Lee Iseli led to the observation that he had been sexually assaulted after death. I would eventually learn more about this.

Cole Neer's trousers had also been pulled down. Strangely, in spite of this gruesomeness, this spoilation of innocence, I could somehow feel the children, beyond the evidence. I became encompassed by an eerie sense of somehow knowing these young victims. I imagined the boys playing and what they were like. I *knew* what they were like. I could actually *feel* Lee's smile. My imagination? Were these kids talking to me from beyond the grave, in a language only I could hear? I never told anyone about my feelings and wondered if C.W. and Dave had had a similar experience. Did my patient, who died and left his body for me to discover the tumor, know in some strange way before he passed on that I would insist on an autopsy? I chided myself: crazy thinking, Turco. You're a psychiatrist. A man of science. Chemistry and physics, not magical thinking. Rationally, I know my thinking stemmed from the repository of anger, guilt and grief that C.W., Dave and I had taken on from being exposed to the sickness of the unnamed homicidal pedophile whom we sought. Our anger and sadness were understandable, our guilt was irrational. Like the idea of original sin, we felt stained, dirtied by the convoluted passion of the killer. We were also aware that we shared our repugnance with the other professionals who confronted life in earnest and expected to face the consequences. There was no question in my mind that the perpetrator was probably fascinated with the killing. The result of my thinking eventually coalesced into a profile of the predator. I was anxious to paint a psychological picture of the man so that all of us could know him in the flesh. So there could be no escape for him. So that wherever he went people would recognize him and be warned.

The development of a psychological profile is a team endeavor encompassing the integration of the crime scene, autopsy findings, witness interviews and reports, photographs and forensic materials. Profiling involves the preparation of a biographical sketch gathered from this information and from known psychodynamic material. The personal habits and relationships of the victim are considered. Sought as a primary objective is fusion of the profiler with the perpetrator and the emergence of a vision of the perpetrator as interpreted by the profiler.

The profile has the purpose of a psychological assessment of the crime scene. Working backward from the crime scene, one attempts to develop a short biography of the outstanding characteristics of the suspect to illuminate and better direct the investigation. The profile is used in conjunction with the physical evidence, recognizing that the homicide scene is a sign of the "acting out" of the perpetrator.

People have always wanted to understand their adversaries, competitors and friends and psychological profiling thus dates back to Biblical times. Lao Tze, in discussing war, understood the importance of understanding one's enemy. The work of Sigmund Freud and the development of psychoanalysis provided a scientific framework for the study and prediction of human behavior. Freud studied a number of well known artists such as Leonardo DaVinci and Michelangelo and produced lengthy profiles of their character. He collaborated with William Bullett and produced a profile of Woodrow Wilson.

The Wilson profile has received great criticism, but much of this work has been substantiated by modern neurological studies. The profile of Wilson has many parallels to a criminal profile in that the same techniques are applied in each case. Historical studies are not the same as detective work, yet they are important for understanding the reconstruction of connections between early life experiences and later behavior. Many modern leaders attempt to keep their early developmental experiences secret because they are aware that foreign governments utilize such information to understand them.

In a psychobiographical profile of a historical figure or world leader, information is known about the person. Psychodynamics — an explanation of psychological behavior — are formulated and an attempt is made to understand the motivations and actions of the person. For example, perhaps Leonardo painted the Mona Lisa because it related to a childhood memory of his biological mother. Perhaps Woodrow Wilson had difficulty with the negotiations at the League of Nations because of early relationship difficulties he had with his father and his own resistance to compromising.

These are working theories that we utilize as best we can. In preparing the profile of a suspected criminal *whom we do not know,* the psychodynamics are utilized to better understand the "identity" of this unknown person. We are working backward in this instance. Psychobiography laid the groundwork for the later development of psychological criminal profiling.

Perhaps more successful, and certainly better accepted, than the Freud and Bullett analysis of Wilson was Walter Langer's study of Hitler, prepared for the Office of Strategic Services during World War II. Langer, a psychoanalyst, was eager to take on the task and was later praised by Winston Churchill. Langer predicted Hitler's death by suicide and described the nature and circumstances under which he would turn his aggression upon the German people, thus anticipating Hitler's orders for the destruction of Germany near the war's end. In essence, Langer developed an understanding of Hitler's repetition compulsion, his tendency to repeat developmental experiences, and used it to predict the dictator's future actions. With the plethora of knowledge we have about criminal behavior, the profile of a criminal is formulated using these data in place of the specific developmental information we don't have. Langer was remarkably accurate and his profile of Hitler remained a military secret until the early 1970s. It was Freud who taught that the *repetition compulsion* is the human tendency to recapitulate as adults our childhood traumas and fears. Unconsciously, we keep repeating our original wounds in thought, memories, dreams and deeds. This is one reason why a person has bad dreams after a traumatic event.

Other notable figures involved in psychological profiling of political leaders have included Harold Lasswell, who ushered in an era of sophisticated psychobiography of historical figures. Jerrold Post studied the effects of the aging process on leadership and the emotional states of terrorists. Erik Erikson's book on Ghandi has become a classic, and it was Bryant Wedge who used a practical application of Erikson's work in preparing a psychological profile of Khrushchev for President Kennedy prior to their Vienna summit meeting. This profile included information on how to negotiate with the Soviet leader during his mood swings and predictions and causes of Khrushchev's behavior.

In the case of criminal profiling, we have had demographic data available since the 19th century. Officials at the Centers for Disease Control (CDC) in Atlanta established a violence epidemiology branch to identify the symptoms of the "disease" of homicide. The FBI has accumulated data based on interviews with serial killers and developed a schema of *organized-disorganized* killers, which is of some help since demographic material of this nature is important in providing a starting point for the project. Until the 1950s and early 1960s, psychiatrists became involved in cases only after a suspect was in custody, for purposes of a forensic court-ordered examination. A New York psychiatrist named James A. Brussel pioneered the use of psychological profiling in the investigatory phase of a case while working with police on the Mad Bomber and Boston Strangler cases. Since then, psychological profiles have gained reluctant acceptance in the law enforcement community and are more commonly utilized.

In the Mad Bomber case, Dr. Brussel reviewed the case file, photographs and many anonymous letters the bomber had mailed over a 16-year period, and suggested to the authorities that they "look for a heavy man. Middle aged. Foreign born. Roman Catholic. Single. Lives with a brother or sister. When you find him, chances are he'll be wearing a double-breasted suit, buttoned." When police arrested George Metesky on January 20, 1957, in addition to matching Dr. Brussel's psychological profile, he was taken into custody wearing a double-breasted suit.

Similar work was performed in the Son of Sam case in New York City. During 13 months between 1976 and 1977, six people were killed and seven wounded by gunshots as they sat in their parked cars. The murderer communicated with authorities by sending cryptic messages to major metropolitan newspapers claiming he was acting under the instruction of a neighbor's dog. Dr. Murray S. Miron, a professor at Syracuse University, was asked to perform a psycholinguistic analysis of these messages. This is a sophisticated form of analysis that reveals clues to the origins, background and psychology of the writer or speaker, in addition to his motivations, personality and psychopathology. The true determination of the perpetrator to carry out his threats can also be ascertained.

Dr. Miron accurately predicted that David Berkowitz, the killer eventually convicted in this case, would be between the ages of 20 and 25. He would be of average height and overweight. His mother was either dead or separated from the family (Berkowitz was adopted and his adoptive mother died when he was 14), and that his father was either ill or aged (he was retired). Dr. Miron characterized Berkowitz's behavior by predicting that he would surrender meekly when confronted by the police and would confess to his crimes.

In the contemporary Unabomber case, the FBI developed a profile that does not appear to have been utilized to best advantage. The profile developed at the FBI Behavioral Sciences department noted the Unabomber to be an "asocial obsessive-compulsive loner of above-average intelligence." He was thought to be from the Chicago area with connections to academe. This profile was developed in 1980 after the fourth bombing attack and 16 years later it proved reliable. One FBI agent was sharply critical of the FBI for setting the profile aside and relying only on "facts." He believed that Theodore J. Kaczynski would have been captured ten years sooner if the profile had been used. Fortunately, agents like Clint Van Zandt have been able to demonstrate the proficiency of psychological profiling in cases such as the Freemen affair in Montana. The director of the FBI, Louis Freeh, viewed this operation as a testing ground for the psychological approach.

Crime profiling must start with something logical and sensible, because simplistic "cookbook" interpretations reduce the efficacy of behavioral scientific profiling and can lead an investigation astray. I look to the uniqueness of a crime scene and then utilize my own unconscious, plus psychoanalysis, for a hypothetical construct regarding the perpetrator.

Psychiatrists use terms like "malignant narcissism," a form of antisocial personality disorder and make predictions based on an understanding of the dynamics of a person thus classified. These are individuals who are sadistic, with strong paranoid tendencies but in good contact with reality. No one has ever successfully treated (cured) a serial killer and psychological treatment is not possible because you cannot *give* a person something he has not developed at the appropriate stage of psychological individuation — empathy and conscience. We can demonstrate this lack in physical medicine when a drug is given to a pregnant mother which produces a deformity in the offspring. With serial killers we have the psychological equivalent of deformity — something has failed to develop.

While working with the task force, I reviewed the data bases available and these included the type of murders, the ages of the victims and type of weapon used. Style of dress, make of car, military history and recreational preferences are important. These help to construct a broad outline of potential perpetrators — not one single individual. The data are available from the Centers for Disease Control, the Violent Criminals Apprehension Program and information we have developed over the years. The FBI system of organized and disorganized murders is helpful.

Organized murderers are methodical and cunning; they are more likely to live with a partner (as was the case with Randall Woodfield, the I-5 killer), to have their own transportation (usually a car in good condition), to be involved in skilled or semi-skilled work, to be socially competent and middle class. Frequently they are only children or among the oldest of their siblings.

An organized crime scene is one in which the victim has been specifically targeted, in which the killer has used restraints and to which a weapon has been carried and then taken away. Organized killers are also excited by cruelty and publicity; they often torture their victims before killing them; and they follow police investigations through the media and by frequenting police haunts to follow the progress of a case — maybe their case. They may also re-visit the crime scene partly to ensure that the body has been discovered, but also to bring back a body part or to "talk" to the victim if his body is still present. Law enforcement officers have learned to "wire" some of the graves of victims of serial killers in the event of the killer's visit to the grave site. Ted Bundy, the so-called All American serial killer, who murdered dozens of women across the United States, typifies the organized serial murderer.

Disorganized murderers are generally mentally disturbed, single, low to middle class, have below-average intelligence, don't have cars, have a history of mental disorder and are employed in menial or unskilled work. Disorganized crime scenes reveal evidence of spontaneity or frenzy, the use of weapons of convenience (to beat or strangle, rather than to shoot), an absence of apparent motive and great disarray, frequently including post mortem slashing, stabbing or mutilation of an exploratory nature. If the victim is penetrated sexually, it is with objects. If the killer re-visits the scene, it is to re-live the experience or to further mutilate the body.

The simplicity of the organized-disorganized classifi-cation is more complicated when we are confronted with a specific case. There are mixtures of these as well as extra-neous disruption of the crime scene and intentional cover ups. An organized murderer may camouflage his crime using disorganized behaviors. Many attempt to disfigure a victim as a means of hiding her (his) identity. It takes training to discern this behavior from the product of a mentally ill person. The psychoanalyst without investigative training would have a difficult time assembling a criminal profile.

A police officer, trained as a profiler does best when he has had psychological training. Crime scene evidence, autopsy findings, blood splatter evidence, witness reports, photographs, psycholinguistic data (if available) and demo-graphic materials must be integrated to develop the initial sketch. A composite personality description also utilizes the biographical characteristics of potential suspects. Many psychiatrists do not deal with criminal behavior at the field level because of the gruesome aspects of the work. Homicide detectives face this almost daily. The situation must also be discussed in plain talk with officers and the profiler working together so that precious time is not lost in the investigation. The legal authority to handle evidence must be considered. The chain of evidence is paramount. Materials are bagged at the crime scene and transferred to police criminalists, pathologists, lab technicians and sometimes prosecutors. Human error or willful tampering can contaminate or compromise the evidence and the legal case it supports. There are strict protocols for personnel handling evidence along the chain into court. With my police training and clinical work serving as a theoretical and practical foundation, I draw upon martial arts training and metaphysical studies for the creative, intuitive process that will guide my reflection. This is not unlike the manner in which I live my entire life. Professional experience and spiritual practice allow for the suspension of conventional reality and the blending of science and mysticism. My own unconscious is my guide.

On an unconscious — semi-conscious — level, I attempt to do what the serial killer does with his victim: fuse and identify. In this state, there are no barriers to under-standing. I am at one with the killer: I intuit his thoughts and feelings, and identify with the rage and frustration that drive him toward acts of violence. As in the case of mythical Native American shape changers, I alter my thinking, change shapes. I will outwit my target: "stealing" his funda-mental self. His path becomes mine. His footsteps my own. I am at one with bow and target.

In the case of the killer of the three boys, we were frustrated precisely because we couldn't define our target. The FBI had already developed a profile, but it was proving useless to the investigation and we would later find out how misleading it was. There wasn't much evidence to point us in the right direction. The children's bodies, their injuries and a few minimal clues as to the weapons used were the sum and substance of our physical information; the killer had left no finger or footprints, no saliva, body fluids or fibers, not the smallest droplet for use in DNA sampling. The children's ages, family histories and places of disap-pearance and death were our only intangible evidence; but we hypothesized that the killer was a stranger to these children and their families so this information was of little direct assistance. In the photographs, Lee's angelic face appeared serene in contrast to the manner of his death. The killer's soul was disfigured. Once again, looking from one photo to another, I felt the presence of Billy, Cole and Lee. "Guide me towards the truth," I said to them in my mind. My meditation and review of the research coalesced into a mental composite. My paper tiger. Our killer was acting out a role written for him in childhood — arrested in develop-ment. Disfigurement — soul dead. He would kill again. I knew that without the slightest doubt or hesitation. My thoughts proved prophetic. There is a David Miller woodcut of Freud that hangs above my desk. Good company for me. It is significant to me because it represents the substantial advances in psychodynamic theory and theory of the unconscious that Freud developed. It serves as an inspiration to me.

In clinical practice, I deal with the outcomes of events and relationships my patients can't remember. Infancy is one such mystery, yet we psychiatrists consider the first three years of life the *separation-individuation phase* of development. These 36 months of development have a major lifelong impact on adjustment, happiness and later behavior. Psychological structure forms in the child largely through his interaction with his parents, influenced by biological events. Understanding these theoretical constructs puts the profiler in the best position to prepare an accurate profile and understand his target. A graduate degree alone is insufficient preparation compared to law enforcement and clinical experience. Of necessity, most profilers are law enforcement officers without clinical training but with knowledge of psychology. The most important factor in my profile work, whether of criminals, artists or historical figures, is a thorough understanding of developmental psychology from a psychoanalytic perspective. Demographic (statistical) data is helpful, but is only a small part of the story.

I prepare by reviewing some basic material on lust murder, primarily the psychodynamics based on modern advancement of ego psychology and our understanding of pathologic malignant narcissism and borderline states. These ideas encompass the field we call object-relations theory. A review of all the known data we have — autopsy reports, crime scene visits, photographs follows. Then a walk alone — perhaps for several hours. Everyone must find his own contemplative path. In my search for truth in life, consideration is given to four categories: religion, psychoanalysis, physics and art. Individually, ideas are related to each perspective. Someone else may find a sweat lodge or vision quest most useful — or perhaps a karate or kendo session.The four components relate to my life and those who touch it. The cornerstone is *religion*. This does not refer to organized religion in the societal sense, but to a search for and interest in the mysteries of life, the creation and development of a moral code and, ultimately, death. This package of beliefs helps to make the world coherent.

The second component, *psychoanalysis* teaches us about the stored beliefs and their influence on our daily lives. Without an understanding of the unconscious, there is no understanding of man. The third component, *physics* provides a glimpse of the ultimate story of life and creation and the structure of the universe. A story we will never know, but approach. The contemporary blending of Eastern mystical beliefs and contemporary physics is not surprising and the similarities of psychoanalysis, physics and religion are so dynamic and powerful that they represent an extension of thought of each discipline. The fourth consideration, *art,* is the category that anticipates physics and graphically illustrates the unconscious. In fact, art speaks a truth of its own — directly from the unconscious. Moral judgment, right and wrong are set aside — fusion and identification occur and conventional reality is suspended as science and mysticism blend. With the task in perspective of these four paths, the work begins. The unconscious leads — freed up from conventional constraints. Perhaps what some officers call a hunch. Perhaps a little more involved.

In creating a profile, the crime scene in its entirety must be considered and viewed as a symptom of behavior and in a broader perspective as a projection of the perpetrator's personality, lifestyle and development. Secondly, the neurological basis of behavior should be considered, especially the recent research on the vegetative nervous system known as the limbic system. Possibilities of such clinical entities as the dyscontrol syndrome should be kept in mind. A large proportion of violent offenders have neurological defects that reflect the nature of the crime scene. Many of these defects are not detected until autopsy. Serial killers may have a predatory drive or compulsion to stalk and kill fueled by neurological defects. This, however, provides no excuse, legal or medical, for such behavior, and we are a long way from understanding the specific significance of neurological findings. The third element in understanding involves the psychoanalysis of behavior and an appreciation of what the killer is actually doing with his own psychological drives, including his attempt to reduce tension by killing, only to be followed by a quiescent period, the buildup of tension and another murder. The profiler's skill is enhanced by an understanding of child development and the later manifestation of defects occurring in the separation-individuation phase.

I draw on a reservoir of experience and knowledge and then try to cultivate what the Zen masters call "beginner's mind" — an empty mind, waiting to fill with the essence of the enemy. The fourth element, demographic data, includes such information as the ages of victim and perpetrator, style of dress, type of weapon used and how, the killer's make of car and known psychiatric histories and data on specific mental illnesses among perpetrators. Most serial killers are not mentally ill in the usual sense of the word, but suffer from a personality disorder reflected by the absence of a conscience, a pleasure in the suffering of others, a desire to inflict the suffering and an absence of ability to empathize with human beings.

With this approach one tries to "get into the mind" of the perpetrator. Inevitably, getting into the mind of the killer has its hazards for the investigator, particularly if he allows himself to become influenced by the darkness he finds. Without a strong sense of himself, the will to resist, the hunter can be overwhelmed by his fear and his morbid fascination with the depravity of the monster's thoughts. Frightened and drawn to evil because, like every one of us, he is uncertain about his own dark side. But we were making progress. We covered a lot of territory. Detectives Trimble and Jensen worked day and night interviewing suspects, family members and following leads. We had covered a lot of psychological territory as well. I was tired. Helpful to me were the writings of Yamamoto Tsunetomo, a samurai who never actually engaged in warfare and Miyamoto Musashi, master of fudo, a form of brush painting, and possibly the greatest samurai ever. Musashi believed that the sword and brush should be wielded with equal precision. We were trying to do this with our investigation and profile. Japanese police still train with martial arts followed by flower arrangement. We wanted to cut through the case with precision — like a properly thrust sword. What I knew haunted me. The killer gained relief from psychological rage by sexually assaulting and killing his victims. He dehumanized them and there would be more deaths. The sense of relief he gained from his last murder would be brief, perhaps less than 30 days separating the episodes. We were running out of time. Little did I know how chillingly accurate our profile would be or how mortal a blow it would deliver to the target.

Before we arrived at our first profile of the children's killer, what came to my mind was a preliminary description. I believed we were looking for a man who had no friends, who had had shallow relationships all of his life, who was basically very glib, at least with regard to dealing with children. He had a gift of gab with kids. He was very selfish. He had his own interests solely at stake. He was looking for total gratification. He possessed an intense sexual curiosity, and would stop at nothing to satisfy it. It was certainly true, I believed, that our killer was a person who had lost the essence of his humanity. Probably because of some deprecatory and repetitive sense of displacement in his childhood, a malevolent transformation gradually took place. When this happens to a human, the soul dies in a very real sense.

With time, I became agitated and depressed. I wondered about people. My car was always parked in the open in downtown Portland. Interior garages are dangerous. Driving home from a task force meeting one day, I passed my favorite bakery and wondered how many child molesters worked there! I thought about the wonderful park near my office. How dangerous it could be. The case was getting the best of me. Who was a closet pedophile? Maybe someone I knew. The techniques I used to get away from this kind of thinking included long-distance swimming and music. Joanne and I were both great fans and contributors of KMHD, our local jazz station. Once, I did a program for them on Duke Ellington. Distractions and diversions, however, can only go so far. I couldn't distract myself.

Driving home one day, I looked up at the surrounding hills of Portland and thought about the normality of the city.

The hills are studded with beautiful, contemporary houses, each unique. Many border on Washington Park and the Wildwood Trail, one of the longest natural woodland trails within U.S. city limits. Washington Park houses the zoo, a science center, the World Forestry Center and the Vietnam Veterans Memorial. There *are* normal people jogging on this trail, walking their dogs, talking to friends — living life. Our own home rises four levels. Five, including the garage level. It's mostly glass — large picture windows and skylights surrounded by sloping wood panels. Sitting in my study, I looked down at the pedestrian traffic. The study is isolated — remote, interior, protected. We are interior people. A doctor of the mind and a woman of books. The world is outside. Our contemporary home contrasts with those of our neighbors. Tudor, Georgian, French Provincial and Italian.They are built on sloping ravines or into the hills.

Ours is a neighborhood of flowers. Rhododendrons, azaleas and roses — as befits the Rose City. I lost sight of the beauty of this scene because my eyes were seeing things and not substance. I was too busy to feel, existing but not living. The person who instructs others on how to live isn't living. I also began to re-live old cases. One in particular stood out in my mind. In the mid-80s, Dave Bishop and I worked on a series of rapes. The eighteenth victim, the only one who had gotten a glimpse of the perpetrator, thought she could help us. The rapist had covered the eyes of the other victims with towels so they couldn't give visual iden-tification clues. We had plenty of voice material though. The 18th victim had a psychological block and would have been a good candidate for Jeanne Boylan, the police artist. She wasn't available, so I hypnotized this woman and our police artist developed a composite sketch as she talked from a relaxed memory. I developed a profile sketch. As a result we tried a lead — a hunch.

Our staff detectives pored through the medical histories of the patients. All eighteen had been patients at St. Vincent's Hospital in Portland during the 18 months previous to the rape attacks! It seemed apparent that someone had access to the women's medical records and their addresses and phone numbers. The timing of the rapes gave further clue to an employee's hours. Curiously, the rapes never occurred on weekends. Perhaps, we thought, the perpetrator was married. Dave, two other officers and I began sifting through personnel records in certain specific clinic areas where the women had been examined. The records led us to a janitor in the medical department who chose his victims based on their medical profiles. He was arrested and convicted.

Another case we resurrected involved a baby who died by drowning. Bishop wouldn't let go of this one. I looked at the autopsy photos and saw a child whose face had been burned — scalded. How did this ever get by the medical examiner? We learned that he had taken the police officer's word that the child had drowned. Dave reopened the case, demoted the officer and finally arrested the boyfriend of the child's mother. He had drowned the baby in scalding bath water because the infant was uncooperative, and convinced the mother it was an accident. This man pled guilty to manslaughter and received a very light sentence. So much for criminal justice — and the baby.

The murders of the three children occupied my mind constantly. My practice suffered. My temper became more apparent. I avoided referrals of new patients. Comfortable with the familiar, I didn't want new challenges in the office. Love can be dangerous, intimacy uncomfortable. Joanne tired of hearing about corpses and police. She left the room when I spoke on the phone. One day she took offense at my wearing my .45 at the kitchen table during lunch. I had come back from a task force meeting and didn't want to take it off. This led to a fight and some name calling. I said she was stupid. In my eyes she was. Joanne didn't understand my crusade. My narcissism was getting the best of me and beginning to ruin a relationship.

She told me what she thought but I wasn't listening. A familiar experience in stressed families. One spouse doesn't hear. There is a *New Yorker* cartoon which speaks to this point. A wife is holding chocolates and flowers and is telling her friend that her husband has been so considerate since she shot him. I was consumed with police and killing. Dinner parties became awkward. What was commonplace to me was shocking to others.

One evening, a casual statement from the wife of a friend prompted a morbid response from me.

She said, "The whole world isn't full of crime, you know."

Scathingly I said, "You could very easily have your throat strangled or be murdered and raped tomorrow."

The guests sat in stunned silence until Joanne intervened with a change in conversation. My non-police friends were getting tired of this — and me.

The strain on our marriage also brought up old unresolved issues. Any long term marriage has little hurts, dissatisfactions, jealousies and slights that ordinarily don't amount to much. It's the "you did, I did" scenario. Part of middle age is working through these issues and laying them to rest, without a compromise in individuality. Sometimes a therapist is needed. The strain of the murder investigation intensified our marital sensitivities. Instead of conversation there were sarcasms, one liners, negativisms.This further strained our social relationships. People took sides, mostly Joanne's. One of her friends told me I was a D-minus husband.

As time went on, I learned more about pedophiles and their community ties. The most visible group is the North American Man Boy Association (NAMBA), an organization formed in the late 1970s, with offices in New York and San Francisco, as well as affiliate branches. This organization supports men and boys who desire sexual relationships. Computers provide information about available children in different parts of the world and advice is proffered to fugitive pedophiles, including legal advice. The acquisition of illegal passports and overseas bank accounts is also on the instruction agenda.

There are some police officers who cruise the Internet in an attempt to solve computer-sex crimes and this has become a selected form of police work. Although interesting, this information wasn't much help to me directly in forming a composite of the man we were looking for. In fact, extraneous information can consume time and lead one astray.

With our investigation, we were in a battle with the clock. When something must be done, and I have the job, I don't question whether it can be done or if I'm the person to do it. It's enough simply to try. If someone else is better qualified, so be it. Let him take on the task. This investigation took on a life of its own. We found many people who fit the category of a pedophile and maybe even a child killer but there were alibis and other circumstances that mitigated against making an arrest

As Lewis Carroll wrote and Alice cried in *Alice's Adventures in Wonderland:* "Curiouser and Curiouser!" My task was very clear. We wanted a profile — a piece of paper with a description written on it. Something that would bite. Something big and tough. A paper tiger!

Evolution of a Tiger

I don't read murder or mystery stories. Recalling past homicides or gruesome events is not in my repertoire and by the time the task force was formed, I had interviewed hundreds of murderers, mostly after their apprehension

However, the gruesome content of arson, murder, hostage problems and man-made trauma takes its toll. The accumulated stresses over the years, so remote from most people, were exerting a strong influence on me. Individuals working as paramedics, firemen, police officers and combat soldiers are especially prone to post-traumatic stresses even years after they leave the job. Human beings are not designed to experience repetitive traumas — the "people pain" — and lead a normal life. Navajos have a cleansing ceremony for soldiers returning from war and this proved very effective with returning Vietnam veterans. In mainstream American culture, the problems of shame, guilt and grief are dealt with by religion, psychotherapy or denial, and mostly the latter. During the intensity of my work, my own denial of physical symptoms and alterations of mood was paramount. By ignoring personal inputs, the fusion with a killer became more facile. Ignoring advice from friends and not asking for any, I worked — asleep and awake.

There is a courage in exploring new ways to experience life, the self and the unconscious. The unconscious is timeless. No isolated past or present, only a fusion of both. As the physicists say, time is elastic and this is no more true than in the depths of our unconscious thought processes. Ambiguity is omnipresent. Facts, techniques and statistics take a back seat to intuition and unconscious dynamics. Training and knowledge are important but only up to a point. As Pasteur once said, "Chance favors the mind prepared." I was working with the elusive "chance," relying without conscious thought on medical and police training. The crime scene is a symptom — a map of behavior, and reflects the early life of the perpetrator. How to read the map? That is always the novel question. This behavioral imprint is a projection of the killer's mind, personality, lifestyle and developmental experiences. The crime scene, understood in totality, "speaks." It speaks not in the language of guesswork, but in the application by the sensitive observer of theory and experience. This is "listening with the third ear," as we say in psychiatry. Looking and listening. Letting go. Understanding moves beyond the obvious and measurable.

But the fact is that I, the physician/cop, no more than any other police officer, can hope to escape the accumulated stress of police work. For that reason, I cannot leave the subject of people pain without acknowledging the harm constant stress and trauma does to the police officer. Without corrective therapy, the human in the uniform with the badge can become twisted, deeply angry and dangerous, if not to others, then certainly to himself.

Bloody crime scenes. Dead mutilated children. Sexually abused and physically maimed children. Young women with bullet holes in their faces and heads. Breasts and nipples cut away and mutilated. Poles stuck through vaginas. Any moderately sensitive person exposed to events such as these over time begins to accumulate a reservoir of people pain.

I wonder, when my mind roams to the past, how the police officers with me on the case of the killer in the walk-in refrigerator dealt with their memories of that terrible murder.

The murderer was a man by the name of Rawlings who is confined to a hospital for the criminally insane. He barged into 7-Elevens and cut the proprietor's throat. Usually this was a woman, a young woman. He would cut her throat then drag her body into the freezer. There, he drank her blood. The police arrested him in the act of lapping up blood from one victim. He had a fetish for tidiness, sweeping the floor of the freezer with a blood-soaked broom.

I was involved in a homicide in which a man disrobed a woman, then sliced open her uterus in which he implanted a crucifix. He spread her arms and legs out in the form of a larger crucifix. That is how police found her.

In my current case, as we strived to develop a profile of the killer of the three boys, I once again began to question life's purpose and the whole idea of human existence. What was the reality, if any, of a personal God? The question somehow tied in with the supreme effort needed for me to get through a day. Was it worth it? It is the accumulation of experiences that finally tips the scale. The scale of ... normality.

I recall one telephone call I received from a young woman asking for my help. She said she had heard I was a kind doctor and she was reaching the end of hope in her life. I had none to give her. I will always regret having to refer her to another physician for care. I simply could not add to my burden, nor could I in all good justice give her the part of me all patients need. This part is the sometime secret life of psychiatrists and especially the secret life of police officers who wear the mask to hide their pain and openly display cynicism and hardness

Behind the leather jackets, the shields, the helmets and the badges there is a core of sensitivity which is defended against and hidden from the "nice people" in society.

I felt I could not shake what finally had been delivered at my doorstep and I felt like an inadequate jerk. Life took on a meaninglessness known only to those who have made the journey into the void. It is a desperate place to be. I felt I could not tune in to a couple who consulted me for marital counseling. I couldn't understand the relevance of their petty bickering about who picks the breakfast cereal. I could not concentrate on what I determined to be nonsense. I had more important problems.

Daydreaming through sessions, I gladly referred such patients to other therapists. I remembered a police officer who had responded to a multiple shooting in the Multnomah County Courthouse. It had occurred during a divorce proceeding. Several people were murdered and the shooter then killed himself. The investigating officer whose duty it was to supervise the crime scene, completed his assigned task, then frantically tried to reach his wife by telephone. Unable to do so, he rushed home. She was still out grocery shopping as he began running his hands and face through her clothing as if this would give him affirmation of her continued existence.

In my state of mind, I could not help but dwell on the growing crime statistics that forecast increasing violence, with no surcease, in our society. Who would have ever imagined that Red Cross workers in foreign fields bringing relief, medicine and hope to injury victims would be fired upon, killed by heartless terrorists whose complete indifference to human life marks the death of the soul? The tempo increases, the death beat goes on, accelerates, as the innocents become victims of a nameless, murderous frustration that spreads like poisonous water.

Chapter 6

Light and Darkness

— · — · — · — · — · — · — · — · — · — · — · —

*The ultimate measure of a man is not where he
stands in moments of comfort and convenience, but
where he stands at times of challenge and contro-
versy.*
— Martin Luther King, Jr.

I had become so absorbed in the investigation of the
dead boys that I was only barely aware of changes in me
that affected Joanne who, with her sensitive intuition,
discerned a deepening darkness in me. I turned away from
her suggestion that we take a vacation. Perhaps the ferry
through the San Juan Islands on to Victoria. That kind of
trip always engendered a special kind of mood — at once
both romantic and mysterious. The fog rolling across the
Straits of Juan deFuca and over the islands envelops even
the most entrenched cynic in a blanket of insouciant
romance. But I demurred. "Too busy right now. Nice, but
maybe later."

A few weeks after this suggestion, she decided to take a two-week vacation visiting friends on the East Coast. It was thoughtful of Joanne to leave me to my preoccupation with the investigation — or so I thought. Making progress on the criminal work and profile was one thing; reading the signs of our marriage was another. Being a psychiatrist with extensive training in marital counseling was no help in recognizing the increasing distance developing between us, or the signs of my wife's discontentment. A day or two after she left, I took a lengthy walk on the Wildwood Trail in the park adjacent to our home. As is customary during these walks, my mind wandered and I began thinking of the Obon ceremony Joanne and I had attended the prior August. There were about four hundred people present in the Japanese Gardens, not far from where I was now walking, yet one could not hear a whisper among this reverent crowd. The aging Buddhist priestess sat at an oblong wooden table that was covered with a white cloth, laden with bowls of food and vases of flowers. She chanted, nonstop, for an hour, while lighted candles in small boats floated on the water of the upper pond, signifying once again the dead ancestors' departure from earth and return to the spirit world. This tradition evolved in Japan between the seventh and fifteenth centuries and by the Edo period was a national custom. As is characteristic of all such ceremonies, it represents both fear and respect for death. The key religious aspect is the tenet that life is eternal. This honoring — *Ura Bone* — gives thanks to Buddha. The celebration lasts three days.

The spirits of deceased ancestors return and leave again like passing shadows in the reflected glare of the candles and lanterns. For a time, the dead are present and mingle with us. Toro Nagashi, the floating of the lighted candles signifies their departure to the spirit world. There is a continuity of this world and the unknown mystery beyond, and what better place to experience this than in Portland's Japanese Garden, high up, overlooking the city landscape.

Now there were spirits of three children that came to my mind — the three murdered boys. Would I think of them at next year's ceremony? Perhaps light three candles for them? Or were they with me now in the park? In Obon, the living unite, for a time, with the dead. I felt a chill, looked up, and saw a large raccoon sitting in a tree, silently observing me. Watching for the slightest of movements. The darkness of his facial mask suddenly triggered a memory. It seems I had been dreaming of caskets — satin lined. For several nights these dream images had been apparent but I quickly forgot them in the morning, dismissing them as residue of the morbid material I was dealing with. Now I recalled the casket images, heavily bronze handled, but not the faces of the sleeping forms inside.

If a patient had reported these dreams to me, I would have immediately recognized the connection — the deeper meaning. The neurotic significance. I had analyzed hundreds of patients' dreams using the free association method and also worked on my own countertransference in these circumstances. That is, my own psychological responses and emotions brought to the surface by a patient's emotional responses. A resonating with the patient's unconscious. But I am not my own psychiatrist and emotional denial and repression encompassed my entire waking life. You cannot, however, cheat the unconscious. The dreams were a direct map to what was happening with me but I didn't read it. The raccoon kept staring, refusing to be frightened away. Feeling ever colder, I decided to go home.

In retrospect, a vision quest might have restored my self awareness, providing an avenue to self exploration and equilibrium. The raccoon did not call my name. No such advantage was forthcoming. The person I saw in the mirror each morning looked the same. No surface indications of trouble — no gale warnings — maybe some turbulence. My police friend Bishop made a comment that my hair seemed grayer, but I hadn't noticed. I knew I was short tempered, even rude, but attributed this to the fact that I had no time to suffer fools. I worked a few other police cases that paralleled the child murders and kept up with my practice, but found myself increasingly annoyed and angry with the criminal justice system. My conversational scope continued to be limited to murders and the only people listening were police friends. I talked too much. The criminals were winning and my role as a doctor took a back seat.

Exposure to evil warps people. I knew this better than others, having treated police officers for emotional traumas after years of repressing their true feelings. Nowhere could some of my police patients find solace. Alienated from family and friends, their wounds were incapacitating and spiritually devastating. After Dave Bishop solved the I-5 killer case and the trial ended, he said, "It was like Vietnam. No flowers, no parade; no one wanted to talk about it." I recall how he looked like hell, shortly before going off to the hospital. My own sense of control and omnipotence led me to believe I was immune to the shocks and aftershocks of this case and the dozens before. How many homicides had I worked on? Kim Singer, a local television newscaster, startled me one day when she commented that I would be living the case over and over for years to come. I dismissed that idea. Police officers who suffer from post-traumatic stress are re-living earlier developmental traumas kindled by more recent stress — a partner killed, a shooting, a particularly gruesome auto accident or a personal family loss. But the stage is set early with histories of parent loss, parental abuse, and dysfunctional family relationships.

In my large, Italian family of origin, children were prized and loved. There was no abuse, alcoholism, drug addiction or bad parenting. I overlooked the parent loss and didn't consider the scar. (William Styron, the writer, discusses somewhat of a similar experience in his early development). Medical training enabled me to distance myself from some of the horrible sights of military service. Always solidly planted, I knew enough to steer a straight course. People told me I was smart. A close woman friend told me she thought I was a genius and Joanne seemed in agreement. How could I go wrong?

A long time after the shouting was over, Dave Bishop would say that looking at me was like looking in a mirror. I was headed in the same direction of despair that he experienced in the Woodfield case — the case of the I-5 killer. Both of my professions kept me on the defensive regarding the disclosure of feelings to myself and others, despite Dave's efforts to open my eyes to the bottom I was headed toward. It seems that no one can help you on the way down or after you hit. Intimacy, family and friends, took a back seat as I barged ahead. In a sense, I was a bigger, badder fighting machine — the way I sometimes had to fight as a child to get ahead and beyond my ethnic background. A Zen warrior, indifferent to life and death, facing death with neither fear nor anticipation — emotionless.

Now my defenses were hostile one-liners and cutting barbs. It's uncanny how I could find a person's weak spot without even thinking about it. Later, my own psychoanalyst marvelled at this behavior, pointing it out over and over again. One example was a physician friend whose professional appearance meant as much to him as his performance. Whenever he put on his white coat in the office or hospital I'd ask if he were going out to sell Popsicles and dubbed him the "Good Humor man." My needling contributed to the dissolution of our friendship. Bad went to worse and I told myself that we hadn't really been close anyway and I didn't need his friendship.

I once wrote a psychobiography of Duke Ellington which included a discussion of his tendency to drive away the people he felt he needed emotionally or professionally — especially emotionally. He would call up his son, Mercer, in the middle of the night, start an argument and call him terrible names, not because he had a legitimate gripe, but because this would provide a face-saving reason for calling. Eventually, he would meet with Mercer, offer him something to eat or drink and use the whole episode as an excuse for getting together. His baiting and badgering were barriers he erected against intimacy and vulnerability, just as I was using teasing and sarcasm to guard against having to accept and express love. I was also using these defenses to discharge some of the hostility and anxiety I was feeling. As Mercer wrote in his biography of Ellington, "Hate is such a luxurious emotion, it can only be spent on one we love deeply."

To a lesser extent we find this behavior among police officers in the so-called wolf pack syndrome. Officers, especially working on a particularly difficult case, will tease one another with comments that seem morbid, tasteless or insulting. This helps to diffuse the tension and rage accumulating through frustrations. Professionals like lawyers and doctors do not deal well with this kind of behavior but it works well with the police officers who don't take it personally. Beneath the teasing is genuine care and respect. I have frequently been teased about a penchant to appear on television or grant newspaper interviews. Some tease me for being unstable, because I'm a psychiatrist. Dave tells me I never pay for lunch!

In early 1995, a group of police officers attended a White House ceremony to honor fellow officers killed in the line of duty. Hundreds of officers in hotels throughout the city lost control of their emotions and began sliding down escalators, smashing glassware, setting off fire alarms and acting in a disorderly and drunken manner. This obnoxious behavior, while not excusable, was an expression of grief, sorrow and fear not appropriately expressed at a nationally televised event. Most officers tell me they are aware that they do not express their feelings directly and have little opportunity to do so if they wished.

Every relationship is ambivalent. As Freud once said: "We love our enemies and even hate our friends." Teasing, constructively expressed, can be flirtatious and engaging. My barbed tongue was sharp, however, and my caustic comments could burn like acid.

When I picked up Joanne at the airport on her return from her trip, one of the first comments I made was a verbal stab at a colleague. She seemed oblivious and smiled it away. Joanne also seemed confident and more self assured, as if she had previously been a little on edge. In the next few days, I sensed a strong determination in her demeanor. Smug was too strong a word, but determination to set herself above insults is probably a good description of her behavior. Joanne was home and the profile of the killer was almost home as well — almost complete.

Not every profile helps to catch a criminal. Sometimes, after great effort, the profile only verifies what we already know or confirms our opinion after a suspect is convicted. This is somewhat like a laboratory or psychological test used for confirmation after a clinical examination has established the likelihood of a specific disease process. In a country where a substantial number of homicides have no substantial motive, especially as they relate to women and children, a profile is at least a starting point. It provides a focus of attention on what is or is not known. It is no substitute for old fashioned detective work but it does serve as the important focus for a hunch.

My attorney, Victor, has referred to the psychopathic sexual sadists who commit such abhorrent acts as monsters and this is as good a term as any. Vernon Geberth teaches us about monsters in his programs on the psychology of evil. The subhuman aspects of such killings associated with sexual mutilation and torture should not be confused with animal-like behavior. Animals kill for biological survival — not pleasure. Serial murderers, while operating in an empathic vacuum, behave to satisfy their own perverted pleasure, and this malevolence, as Geberth has noted, is incomprehensible without a concept of a psychology of evil. Perhaps, as I suggested earlier, this evil is a reflection of something inside all of us — the monster within. Perhaps, in part, my deterioration was a reaction to my recognition of this monster. Make no mistake about it, most of us will never cross the line — the line of evil. We are not made that way. While some may break the Fifth Commandment, such a decision is entirely different from the sexual sadism we were addressing.

I drink lots of black coffee or diet Coke when I work, and coming back from a walk, I set my ideas on paper and complete my focused task. Kekule, a famous scientist, discovered the structure of the benzene ring while asleep in a hotel room. He had a slight fever and envisioned snakes dancing around and arranging themselves in a six-sided figure. A major triumph in organic chemistry, the unconscious at work. Richard Feynman worked out his equations of quantum thermodynamics in a topless bar he frequented three or four times a week. He sat in the back, drank orange juice and did his calculations on the small napkins provided. We allow our knowledge to simmer. In college I would "sleep" on a problem, only to find the solution near at hand when I woke up. No place for alcohol — no wine until the task is done. Samurai warriors prepare for battle in a similar manner.

    I took the pot of coffee three levels down to my desk, set it on the side and sat in my straight-backed ramrod chair. And I wrote and wrote and wrote.

    Our offender would be a white male between the ages of twenty five and thirty-five years. He would be "alienated and non-affiliated" with groups or organizations. A "cardboard cutout." A Turco term. In essence, a loner.

    The offender probably would have been kicked out of the military service had he served. He would keep close tabs on the investigation and possibly try to assist the police. He would most likely keep records of his crime, including a diary and a compilation of newspaper clippings. His pornography would be child pornography. The offender would keep photographs of his victim. He would possibly use a Polaroid-type camera and most certainly keep post mortem photographs of his victim. He would likely not have a late model car and would be employed at a job with limited responsibility. The offender would have a fetish, a souvenir used for later masturbation and reliving of the sex and murder sequence. The souvenirs would include locks of hair, jewelry and possibly, but not likely, yet in this case, a body part. The child's underwear would probably be kept as a trophy and masturbation fetish. This offender would likely stalk and kill male victims, and probably viewed females as defective and worthy of only secondary attention. A homosexual fixation was apparent furthering the likelihood of male victims.

Control is a primary motivator, with curiosity taking precedence to sexual gratification. This offender was probably transitory with frequent moves. He would continue to kill children and become more brazen in the process, perhaps to the point of dissecting a child. He probably has a history of prior arrests for sexual molestation and a history of mental health counseling. He probably has a lengthy history of deviant sexual behavior which he has hidden with family help, and commonly uses restraints on his victims. He experienced conflict in childhood that had perverted his psychological development. Most probably he killed in a purposeful fashion rather than in a rage. I might never discover the full psychodynamics but, most probably, he felt *psychologically abandoned during his latency years. The problem was more subtle than his being a product of family chaos or violence as it is with men who kill adult women.*

His parents most likely never expressed their own rage and the perpetrator's "acting out" was partly an unconscious mechanism to serve his parents' hidden wishes.

Symptoms of fire setting, bed wetting and cruelty to animals were no doubt a precursor to his more aggressively noticeable behaviors. This triad is helpful in profiling serial killers. He was psychologically primitive, protecting his ego with childlike defenses — overt expressions of rage yet detached from the feeling state. A robotic killer. The mechanism of "splitting" was probably operative with the killer splitting off the good and bad parts of himself. He probably selected his victims as representing himself at certain ages and projected his own personality onto these children, killing off the "badness." I was sure he was not deranged and would know the difference between right and wrong. I knew he could control his behavior and understood the consequences of violating the law. This is one reason he took such pains to evade detection. It is probable that he killed his last victim, Lee, to avoid apprehension. He took a knife to the park, prepared to kill Billy and Cole for the same reason. He took Lee's body to a remote location for the same reason. Yet, he would definitely not be wracked with guilt. His motivation was selfish — narcissistic. No conscience. Serial killers who murder for their own pleasure and sexual perversion have a form of severe personality disorder — malignant narcissism. They have paranoid tendencies, are sadistic, enjoy the sadism and lack empathy for others and a concept of self. They are cardboard people, unable to value the lives of others. No empathy for the victims. They brutalize and torture in an emotionally detached manner. This lack of remorse would allow the killer to hold down a job, and we would find he had one when and if apprehended. He would appear normal, if distant, to co-workers or neighbors. He might present himself as timid, maybe even insecure. Even doctors who may have examined him in the past may have viewed him as being phobic or schizoid, terms doctors like to throw around. An explanation of his fantasy life, however, would reveal these appearances to be a defense against the sadism he was hiding. Social isolation would take precedence over his secret fantasy enjoyment and the eventual acting out of the fantasies. With the success of one or more murders, his depravity would intensify and escalate.

I concluded: *He murdered Billy and Cole as a means to escape detection and planned the murder of Lee for the same reason. A more methodical planning. Lee was in the hands of his killer for a longer period of time. Billy's near escape may have taught him to exercise more control. This was one of several reasons for him to use restraints on Lee, which we believed he did. Our killer had sexual relations with Lee post mortem — necrophilia. This also meant the killer held a morbid fascination and derived as much pleasure from slow killing as he did from the sexual assault. I hypothesized that he killed Lee slowly and engagingly. There would be a next episode more brazen than the ones we knew. He would relieve the tension and rage accumulating between acts of violence, once he learned this was possible and under his control. The sense of relief would be lessened with each murder and the violence would escalate in a vicious cycle. Serial killers are in the "grip of hatred," to use the Dalai Lama's phrase. The negative actions of our killer were an expression of this hatred. The killer was acting out his fantasies.*

We had described our killer and anticipated his next move. Now ... how to catch him?

I was becoming increasingly introspective with the entire serial killer business.There is something inside killers that reflects our morbid curiosity about ourselves, whether we want to admit it or not. It's part of our own monster set. Killers are doing their job — their work as they see it. Nothing unusual — business as usual. No guilt. No remorse. No big deal. Just don't get caught. My job entailed following the killer's reality as well as my own, but this wasn't my only case at the time. I went back to this particular crime scene a few more times. We only knew of one crime scene and one "dump site" at the time. If only the silent earth could talk, speak aloud to what it had witnessed.

Once, on an Air Force 141, I studied Harry Lee Parker's book: *Clinical Studies In Neurology*. This remarkable book is a masterpiece of descriptive science and objective observation. I memorized the book, and its pages continue to be an inspiration and a mnemonic device for me. It is a resource for deductive reasoning in the style of Arthur Conan Doyle — set in the British Isles. This book is one of my bibles and I am never far away from it. Psychiatrists, neurologists and homicide detectives are, at least ideally, seekers of the truth. What we do with the truth may differ, but ultimately we become engaged in the battle — the front line of the spirit. No back seat. Spiritual truth follows. Where would this killer go? Would he fail the company of men? His inability to form attachments was chronic. How does such a person navigate through life? What was his body size? A police buff like Jack Ruby? We had developed about as much of the mosaic as we were going to. A slippery continuum of truth. Crazy James? Crazy Tony? Not likely. This case was not like the U.S. mail bombing cases I had worked on. They involved the bombing of abortion clinics by mail. They proved to be good examples of how psychological profiles can assist investigators in pursuing suspects. My role was analyzing the manner in which a package bomb was tied, the type of lettering, the style and number of stamps used for mailing, the style of paper and the type and amount of bindings used on the parcel.

We can, from such clues, sometimes hypothesize the nature and intent of the bomber; for example whether the bomb is the work of a religious fanatic or neo-Nazi person or group.

Each crime has its unique dynamic perspective. In the case of the three murdered boys, we had no psycholinguistic material to help us. No phone call as with the Atlanta Olympics bombing scenario.

I'm a true believer in psychiatry. Psychiatry heals. Psychiatry relies on science and humanity. It is not a cold, distant discipline but a human, warm and engaging clinical relationship. I had had the benefit of an analysis in the true sense of the word. Many people think psychiatrists all undergo a self analysis, but that is not true. Only a handful of psychiatrists go on for a psychoanalysis, which is quite costly in terms of time and money. It usually involves lying on "the couch" for one hour from three to four times a week. Far from an idle preoccupation with the self it is very hard work. The analysand — the patient — must free-associate to everything in his life, including dream material and personal, secret fantasies. One's entire inner life is laid bare for examination and, in the process, one recapitulates past traumas great and small in the context of the analytic relationship. The corrective emotional experience. One need not like one's analyst for this process to work, and in fact the analysand frequently transfers rage experienced at earlier times of life with parental figures to the person of the analyst. The feelings must be examined and traced to their origins. These feelings are the result of "pressure" from the unconscious out of one's awareness and also reflect pre-verbal experiences. Infants have feelings that are stored in their brains long before they have the ability to conceptualize verbally.

This is very important and these pre-verbal issues are dealt with in a special way in analysis with specific theoretical models of understanding. Far from analysis being a lucrative job for the analyst, it is hard work for him and entails major responsibilities. Although psychoanalysts earn a good living my opinion is that the patients get the best deal. A good analysis can undo a lifetime of misery and also serve to prevent a future lifetime of misery. A good analysis can cure some physical illnesses and certainly ameliorate others. In my case, I learned a great deal the first time around and also dealt with heavy emotional content. However, I was becoming increasingly aware of the re-emergence of unanalyzed material exerting an emotional impact on my life. Even my writing was full of anger — physically angular and scribbled.

The night we concluded work on the profile, I had a nostalgic dream. The original dream that convinced me of the need or at least the desire to enter analysis was one of Edvard Munch's "The Scream," a painting of a face contorted in pain and protest. The embodiment of grief and desperation. Inside me there was something I wanted to scream about. I placed this image, in the dream, outside my childhood home. This was worse than death. The foreboding of soul death. I worked on this dream and related issues in my initial excursion into analysis and viewed the experience as a professional as well as personal accomplishment. I was doing what many could or would not do. When I was ten years old, my father took a year to die of lung cancer. This was a year of agonized suffering during which time he endured cobalt treatments and their side effects. He ate mush, lost weight and slowly strangled to death.

After his loss, I became cachetic — anorexic. I became a skeleton, was pronounced by a physician to be undernourished and had to be force fed. Undernourished in an Italian family! No one made the connection. Remaining slender throughout my life, weight gain was something of a priority with me and an equation with health.

Now, with the accumulation of homicide cases, and the murder of children, two of whom were the same age I was at the time of my father's death, and my weight ordeal, I was re-living a childhood experience. I didn't recognize this at first. I was dogged with a continuing lousy feeling and the behavioral symptoms which were becoming ridiculous. My illusions, or more properly, my defenses were breaking down. I knew they were, but didn't know why. My symptoms became absurd. One night while I was out with friends, I had too much to drink, spilled food on my tie and slept through the latter part of the evening. A week before, I had gone to see the movie *Lies My Father Told Me* and became so tearful that it was not possible to stay in the theater. My reaction clearly exceeded the screen material as sad as it may have been. Around this time, I also went fishing with a friend and his father. The absence of my own father represented a significant longing and pain — in my throat, where my father's cancer began. Then the dream! *I was crawling into a casket with my father.* This was the connection with the "casket dreams" and the children. My dream was a symbolic expression of a childhood conflict between the desire to die and go with my father and never lose him, in a sense forestalling his death — and a defense against that desire. To live. Some people keep inside the image of the deceased loved one and eventually develop a psychosomatic illness or depression because they "don't give up the ghost."

Fortunately, I had an opportunity to work on these issues, initially with my own introspection and dream work beginning when I was seventeen years old, later in psychiatric training and still later in a more formal analysis. The dinner episode, my increasing lousy feeling, the marital distancing, the movie issue, my sense of loss and longing during the fishing trip and finally the casket dream — so explicit in nature — convinced me that my childhood loss was still raw. My loss or losses were being re-kindled. The serial killer — still a phantom, but real — was the engaging key to my increasing morbidity. Traumatic incidents are more than perceived disasters, they are opportunities to heal and to do penetrating creative work. I did not blame anyone else for my destructive behavior, even apologizing to my dinner companions. I needed a deeper perspective of the mess I was making of my life. Psychologically bleeding, I faced the music. Although Joanne held my hand and I took fresh showers during sweaty nights of restless sleep, I knew that love was not enough. The healthy part of my ego was asserting itself. Time to be happy or try to become happy. Back to analysis. I called Alex, my analyst, and set up an appointment.

But I knew that while Alex could help in a professional manner, I needed a close friend who could be both sympathetic but detached enough to steer me away from the deep hole I was circling. Then, I remembered Chuck Taylor and a morning with dawn breaking over the sea.

"Can we make it, Chuck?" I yelled, trying to be heard above the voice of the ocean. I tried to sound calm. In near gale winds we were standing on the edge of a small vessel, getting ready to jump into the North Pacific Ocean, or more properly, onto a submarine in the North Pacific Ocean. I was told to keep both my arms outstretched flying through the air, but this is not a natural body movement and the tendency is to put at least one arm down.

Suddenly, I could barely make out the awesome image of the black, cigar-shaped object pitchrolling in the turbulent sea. A sleek tower loomed toward the sky. It was raining and I was wet and cold. Before us was the *U.S.S. Pogey,* an attack class nuclear submarine. As befits a career naval officer, Chuck's response was brief and concise:

"Affirmative!" I knew that he knew that we would be okay — that I had the judgment and ability to execute this operation. He was behind me if anything went wrong, like the time he parachuted over North Carolina when his aircraft engine caught fire.

Halfway between the tug and the submarine I could make out two divers attached to the black cigar with lanyards. If we missed the jump, one or both would unhook for a rescue and there was no doubt in my mind that these men would do their best to save us or die trying. This dedication is especially noticeable with submariners, carefully selected for physical and psychological stamina and dedication. No crybabies on this job. I was afraid, but made the jump holding my breath during the flight. Instantaneously, each diver grabbed one of my arms and motioned, above the roar of the sea, for me to go down the hatch, a circular hole with a halo of light shining through. As soon as I reached the ladder, Chuck was behind, and moving quickly we climbed down an endlessly long ladder without any back support, moving from darkness to light. Once down, we found ourselves ushered into the galley to waiting mugs of hot coffee. The skipper greeted us along with his executive officer. Their smiles could melt an iceberg and I was extremely thankful for the hospitality. And I was grateful for Chuck Taylor's confidence in me.

Many years and adventures later, we remain close friends helping one another with life's adversities. I helped him bury both parents and he's solved not a few of my problems. Chuck was a police officer before his navy days, and would have been of invaluable psychological support to me during the investigation. But he was not available, at least not in person, having moved to California a few years before. We kept in close touch and he visited as much as possible but I was caught up in the details of my life and was not about to share freely. Besides, it was all too complicated; I was restless and confused, but he would have understood even my resistance to ask for help and that would have been a comfort.

Chapter 7

Soldiers

— · — · — · — · — · — · — · — · — · — · — · — · — · — · —

God guard me from those thoughts men think
In the mind alone,
He that sings a lasting song
Thinks in marrow bone
      – Yeats
      King of the Great Clock Tower

Vancouver, Washington, not to be confused with the same named city in British Columbia, lies opposite Portland across the Columbia River. It it known in the Pacific Northwest for its relaxed pace, friendliness, lush vegetation and proximity to good steelhead fishing on the Kalama. It is sometimes jokingly, but only jokingly, referred to as "the other Vancouver." We love the sense of history there, the updated, though small, army base and the ease with which one can hop a small flight at Pearson Airfield for some aerial sightseeing. Not too long ago, Joanne, our friends the Scotts and I had breakfast in the Grant House, former headquarters of Ulysses S. Grant. His command post is now a tourist attraction, complete with original furniture and numerous photographs adorning the walls. Sitting on the rocker on the front porch, we looked out over the parade field and sipped coffee. At the time U.S. Grant was stationed at Fort Vancouver, it was part of the Oregon Territory. During the winter of 1852-1853, the territory was divided and everything north of the Columbia River became Washington Territory. Little did I know as I pondered the colorful past of Vancouver in a relaxed fashion that my memories of the city across the Columbia would be tainted by the sadistic murders of three boys.

On our visit to the Grant House with the Scotts, not only did we learn a little about Ulysses S. Grant's history, but we discovered an anecdote involving an army general who arrived at Vancouver barracks long after Grant had departed to become a bold figure in Civil War history.

This was General George C. Marshall, chief of staff during World War II, Secretary of State, Secretary of Defense and founder of the Marshall Plan which accorded him the Nobel Peace Prize, the first ever given to a military person. He was a brigadier general when he was posted to Vancouver barracks in 1936 and was in an excellent position to deal with an unusual event in history — an event that would literally set down in his back yard.

On June 18, 1937, three Soviet aviators set out to make history. They took off from Moscow in a specially designed aircraft known as the *March of Stalin* to make the first non-stop flight from Europe to America over the North Pole. It was at least as dangerous as Lindbergh's solo flight across the Atlantic ten years earlier. At the North Pole, the aviators encountered bad weather, which created insurmountable problems in flight. Even their water froze. The radio didn't always work, their oxygen supply was used up and they were dangerously low on fuel. They radioed San Francisco that they would have to make a forced and premature landing. When the plane set down in Vancouver, these men were greeted by a Pennsylvania boy become general. George Marshall and his wife, Katherine, became hosts and the general took charge. When the aviators asked for cognac while sitting in the bath tub, Katherine, a proper woman of the day, knew how to handle the situation. The following evening, amidst congratulatory calls from Joseph Stalin, President Roosevelt and world-wide dignitaries, a worldwide radio conference was held in the Marshall home. Even at this early time, Marshall's superior diplomatic skills were obvious and he received commendations from Washington. He handled an impromptu potential disaster with aplomb, diplomatic dignity and warmth. Nevertheless, he regarded himself as a country boy who regretted leaving Vancouver to become Chief of Staff of the Army.

I later thought briefly of Marshall, the man of consummate sophistication and sterling character, when I got involved with the killer whose personality was such a terrible confusion of lust, cleverness, depravity, warped sexuality, selfishness and the overwhelming urge to inflict pain. How could, I asked myself futilely, there be such a remarkable difference in two human beings? — one a generous, delightful, self-effacing man, the other, a warped person devoted entirely to his own secret gratification who was unable to feel sensitivity or compassion for another person's hurt or pain. It was, indeed, a futile question, only a passing thought, it was unanswerable.

Chapter 8

Cole and Billy

—·——·——·——·——·——·——·——·——·——·——·——·——·——·——·——·——·——

Part 2:

Music heard so deeply that it is not heard at
all, but you are the music while the music lasts.
– T.S. Eliot

The Labor Day holiday of 1989 began in a festive
mood for Chief David Bishop, his wife, Patty, and Joanne
and me. We attended a hosted party at one of Oregon's
beach resorts and spent the weekend relaxing on the beach
and teasing one another at an evening wine tasting.
Unknown to us, a man named Westley Allan Dodd was
planning his "kill." I was not to hear his name until
November 13.

Cole Neer and his brother Billy had an extra day that
holiday weekend and decided to spend it riding their BMX
bikes through their new neighborhood of McLoughlin

Heights in Vancouver. A favorite pastime and "business" of the boys was scavenging for golf balls at the Vanco driving range. Some days they found as many as 200 between the two of them and they would sell them back to the proprietor for a penny each — a good way to support their baseball card collecting. We have a psychiatrist friend who lives by a golf course and collects the balls for use in artistic pursuits. It was a given that Cole and Billy would be together — as the sun will shine. Cole was 11 and Billy was 10, and their birthdays were a little over a year apart. The boys were inseparable and industrious. Two peas in a pod, they were the kind of children you would want in your son's Cub Scout den or as your neighbor boys, your paper boys, or mowing your lawn — or perhaps for your children or grandchildren. It was because of their likability that it was so difficult for the police officers who became involved in the investigation of their deaths. We could all feel close to these angels. There were some differences between them. Billy was a prankster and mischievous. He was always ready with a joke or a trick. Cole was more serious. He was the oldest brother and took his position quite seriously. "Why?" was one of his favorite expressions. Cole expected answers and explanations. They were "all American boys." They were also Native Americans. Even if faced with a situation they knew to be unfair or possibly immoral, they would apologize. In 1993, I met their father, Clair, and could still envision the grief etched on his face. He helped me to understand the boys. They were agile and athletic and appreciated their close relationship. They were loyal to one another, rode their bikes together, walked together and shared their fantasies and secrets.

Cole and Billy were just becoming accustomed to their new house. Two months earlier, in the middle of the summer, their dad Clair Neer had abruptly moved the family from their home of three years, in nearby Hazel Dell to the austere — perhaps dreary — slate gray duplex at 305 Council Bluffs Way in the Skyline Crest project. Skyline Crest was low-income housing run by the Vancouver Housing Authority, a non profit agency that received federal funding to help out families like the Neers — families down on their luck. The project spread all along cul-de-sacs and roads off Mill Plain Boulevard on one of the low ridges of the Columbia River Valley. The housing was strictly utilitarian, one step above a trailer park and not unlike the "projects" near my boyhood home in Philadelphia

The boys were probably too young to realize they had come down in the world, but their father was painfully aware of it. He had moved the family all over the Northwest and the northern Great Plains, to places like Priest River, Idaho and Moorehead, Minnesota, looking for work and a home. There were four in the family: Clair, Billy, Cole and Richard, the youngest, who was six years old. Clair Neer had been trained as an auto-glass installer but work was not readily available, especially in the Vancouver area where they had been living for three years. He worked only intermittently, some might say sporadically. He brought the family to the Columbia River Valley at the suggestion of Fast Horse, one of his oldest friends and a Sioux Indian he met while growing up on the Neer family wheat farm in Oberon, North Dakota. Fast Horse was a journeyman carpenter, and had been best man at Clair's wedding to Arlene Neer. Arlene was Cole, Billy and Richard's mother.

Fast Horse told Clair that he always seemed to find work in the Portland-Vancouver area and the advice came at the right time. Clair and Arlene's marriage had just dissolved in bitter acrimony, and Arlene relinquished custody of the children to Clair. Clair was a model father, providing positive emotional and physical support for the children and encouraging their close relationship. Family. As a result, the children were highly thought of in the neighborhood, in spite of financial difficulties. The entire family was admired. Billy and Cole were in the fourth and fifth grades at Marshall Elementary School near McLoughlin Heights. They were good students and rarely missed classes. Cole showed artistic talent at an early age and Billy evidenced an analytic mind and a natural curiosity.

As far as Clair was concerned, the less said about Arlene Neer the better. The divorce had been acrimonious. As Clair described it: "kind of bad." The boys had had no contact with their mother in three years and this was absolutely acceptable to Clair. He knew that Arlene was a poor influence on the boys. She was crossed out of their lives as much as possible. Arlene was a full-blooded American Indian, a member of the Devil's Lake Sioux tribe from northeast North Dakota. A hardy people. Perhaps the boys' athletic ability stemmed from their Native American background. Certainly some of their physical characteristics were inherited from their mother. They all had a bronzed, exotic cast to their features and people were always asking Billy and Cole if they had Oriental blood in them. As a result of Arlene's heritage, all the Neer boys were automatically enrolled as members of the Devil's Lake Sioux. The tribes were on the move so to speak, leasing mineral and oil rights, running gambling casinos and making property investments. At some point, this heritage would be important.

Clair, himself, was brawny — muscular and a little rough, but a real gentleman. He had cobalt blue tattoos snaking up both forearms. He didn't have much money, no expensive "toys" but he loved the boys. "A wonderful, caring father who gave his love and his time freely," said Betty Ahern who was the Neers' landlady when the family lived in Hazel Dell. "He was a father raising three boys by himself. I've never seen a man to spend so much time with children as he did," Ahern said. Obviously, this fathering paid off — Cole and Billy were super good kids. They were, however, to become what I call "double victims" — maternal loss and later total loss. Billy and Cole loved McLoughlin Heights because of the large, sprawling park north across Mill Plain Boulevard from the Skyline Crest development. David Douglas Park was 68 acres stretching east from Andresen Road all the way to Garrison Road. The eastern half of the precipitous site had been developed and given over to ball fields and Cardboard Hill, a sledding run where the kids took pieces of corrugated boxes down in the wintertime. Another use for grocery-vegetable boxes, reminiscent of my own childhood adventures.

The western half of David Douglas had been left just as it was. The Bonneville Power Administration ran a high-line through it, and over the years people had beaten back the brush for a series of trails. The Clark County Track Club used the crude dirt pathways in the park's west half for trail running. This is very common in Oregon and Washington parks. The trees and undergrowth were high, however, as a result of the heavy Northwest rainfall.

This whole section of the park had a wild feel to it and the Neer boys were attracted to it. The paths, mysterious and dark, are much like the ones near my home, in the arboretum. The paths were excellent for biking, especially the kind Cole and Billy loved. They could let go here and mountain bike to their hearts' content. They knew the dips, turns and jumps almost by memory and liked the "getaway" sense and solitude that David Douglas offered them. Skyline Crest was filled with people and this was their escape. They could be alone together. Someday they might grow up to be heroes. As Martin Luther King Jr. once said, "a sleeping hero in every soul."

On Labor Day weekend of 1989, Westley Allan Dodd stalked more than twenty children in sprawling David Douglas Park, near his home in Vancouver. He had come to the park planning murder, and labeled his forays there as "the hunt." He became frustrated, however, because all the children he marked as targets either eluded him or had an adult accompanying them. Cole Laverne Neer, and his brother William James were tragically different. Dodd was able to lure them to a secluded wooded area by ordering them imperiously off their bikes. After molesting one of the brothers, he stabbed both of them to death with a knife he had brought along for the purpose.

The following weekend, across the Columbia, September 9 was a day I spent with firearms training and on September 12, the advanced police academy began. On September 16, a reception was held at the City of Newberg for members of the police force.

But police as a whole were stymied in their massive manhunt for the killer of the Neer boys. Two months later, just before Halloween 1989, Dodd struck again. He kidnapped five-year-old Lee Joseph Iseli from a playground in Southeast Portland. He took the boy home and, after a night of staggering depravity, strangled the child. He sodomized the corpse and left Iseli's body, naked and face up, in a scrub forest, to be found two days later by a pheasant hunter. By October 30, Sergeant Larry Nevill and homicide detective C.W. Jensen were deeply involved in the investigation of the murdered boy. The viciousness of the Lee Iseli murder had drawn a massive police response but was not necessarily seen as part of a pattern of serial killing.

Abernathy, the hunter who discovered Lee's body did not disrupt the crime scene, which was investigated by detectives Dave Trimble and Rick Buckner of Vancouver, and C.W. Jensen of Portland. It was Buckner who noted the reddish discoloration on the victim's neck and I, who had been called in, noticed this very clearly on the crime scene photographs. It was still markedly evident in the autopsy photographs. This, in my opinion, was a ligature mark. An examination of the child's body revealed he had been sexually assaulted. He had sustained damage to his anus and there were lacerations in the pudendal area. There clearly had been anal penetration and internal lacerations. Lee had been sodomized and I was to learn about this first hand.

The Neer brothers had been stabbed. Lee Iseli was strangled. The coroner's investigation failed to uncover evidence of Cole Neer being molested and there was clear evidence that Lee Iseli had been sexually assaulted. Some officers believed these murders were the work of two different killers. I never wavered in the belief that they were the work of one depraved human being. We followed every conceivable lead and there were many false leads. Jensen visited the playground with Justin, Lee's brother, and also interviewed Justin's friends. He tried being supportive with the boy who not only sustained the loss of his brother but also was feeling guilty since he usually watched over Lee. A young child cannot outwit a serial killer.

Chapter 9

Lee

What we call the beginning
is often the end.
And to make our ends
is to make a beginning.
The end is where we start from.
 – T.S. Eliot

Lee Iseli was five years of age at the time of his death. I was to learn more about the gruesome details of this event at a later time and, face to face with horror, I was changed by the experience. He was a charming child, exuding grace and lovableness only a five-year-old could. One might have an image of him some day being a ladies' man; a "cute hunk" as some women might say. He might have become an attorney, a doctor, a policeman or an army general, perhaps like Grant or Marshall who once were stationed at the Vancouver barracks not far from his home, or from his final resting place — the "dump site."

Lee was never to achieve his full potential. Another "double victim" he was to become a trophy in a four-by-six-inch photo album kept by Westley Allan Dodd. This was a dime store photo album I later came to possess. The photos had captions written in by Dodd and cross references to his diary entries which were kept in a separate book. Some of the photographs were taken of Lee fourteen hours after his death and gave clear evidence of post mortem sexual involvement. We had predicted the existence of such material in preparing the profile. Dodd's attorneys would later make a motion to suppress such photographs because they did not want to "incite" jurors into hating Dodd. There is no place for emotion in the courtroom. At least not when it hurts the defense.

Lee had a very good relationship with his brother, Justin, who conscientiously watched over Lee. No one could or would have expected him to outwit a child pedophilic killer. The last time Justin saw Lee was when they played at the Richmond School playground. Lee had separated from his brother to play on the "volcano," a mound of earth the children compared to Mt. St. Helens which blew its top in 1980.

Lee was about three feet, eight inches tall and weighed about thirty pounds. He had blond hair that grew over his ears with bangs in the front. On the day of his disappearance, Jensen learned that Lee was wearing a gray warm-up jacket and tan colored trousers. His brown leather shoes were later to be burned by Westley Allan Dodd in the garbage can next to his apartment. I was one of the people who found them, early one dark morning.

Lee and his brother Justin lived with their father, Robert Iseli, an engaging and emotionally responsive man.

Robert, whom I was later to meet, had been separated from Lee's mother since February of 1986. Robert's mother was also a member of the household, further ensuring that the children received good guidance and care. Their own mother, Jewel, had little if any contact with the children, but Lee did visit his maternal grandparents from time to time. On those days, Justin accompanied him.

My ultimate confrontation with what we might call "the death scenario" brought up an intimate portrait of Lee and a psychological involvement I fostered to better understand the situation, especially in the event that courtroom testimony would be needed. All of what I knew about the children was learned prior to the arrest of a suspect in their murders. The more intimate character, behavior and last moments and hours of death of the children I gleaned directly from my interrogation of the suspect. One thinks of blame in these instances, cause and effect and prevention. What could have been done to prevent this catastrophe? Much later I learned that some of Dodd's former "therapists" actually gave him ideas on molesting children. The criminal justice system, acquainted with his record as a pedophile, let him pass time and time again as slick defense attorneys argued his case for leniency. He was so well known in the court system that some judges, fearing criticism, have refused to come forth to discuss their rulings and involvement in his past offenses. As Robert Iseli was later to state: "There is a lot of blame to be put onto people; none of that blame will bring my boy back, but unless we open our eyes, there will be a lot of other little boys this will happen to."

In an interview after Dodd was arrested, one of his neighbor's, Pansy Swaney, who lived across the street from the apartment Dodd was renting, made a brief statement. She said she had seen a small blond boy who was no older than her six-year-old grandson enter Dodd's residence with him. She said he was wearing a lightweight jacket that appeared to be tan or khaki in color. She further stated: "My feelings are asking me now if this was the Iseli child. I don't even want to think about it."

Chapter 10

The Media

— ▪ — ▪ — ▪ — ▪ — ▪ — ▪ — ▪ — ▪ — ▪ — ▪ — ▪ —

Kim Singer is a superb human being, an attractive blonde and a professional newswoman. We first met in 1977 when she worked as co-anchor on a morning television program. I was a guest, having been asked to discuss clinical depression. Prior to this time, my experience with the media had been positive but limited to Armed Forces Radio and a few civilian television appearances. I found myself very much at ease with television appearances and believe they serve an important educative function. My perspective of television news is that it should be an extension of the classroom in courses such as civics, current events, history and science, albeit in a limited time sequence. Over the years, my appearances on television and media presentations reached the hundreds along with some radio programs. Some of my favorite colleagues in New York and Los Angeles have had similar positive experiences.

When President Reagan was shot by John Hinckley in

March of 1981, I was asked to remain in the newsroom of KPTV to help narrate the unfolding events and to discuss the type of person who might shoot a President and what the consequences might be for the nation and the people. The emotional consequences surrounding the loss of a national leader can be devastating and undermine morale in significant ways. My interest in psychobiography and politics was well known in the community by this time and led to ongoing requests for appearances.

In March 1981, I was driving to a residential treatment facility on a very rainy day when the news of the President having been shot came over the car radio. My own thoughts naturally turned to the place I sat in medical school class when the professor tearfully announced that John F. Kennedy had been assassinated. Then followed Martin Luther King Jr. and Robert Kennedy.

A happier time was when we did the special program on Duke Ellington on KMHD radio, the jazz station. I think of this as the most pleasant of personal media experiences.

The case of the children was another matter, however. David Simpson, the Portland Police Bureau spokesperson asked that I appear on a television program to help assuage community fears regarding a child serial killer and perhaps to give parents some advice on how to protect their children, something every good mother knows better than I. My first meeting with Simpson actually occurred many years before when he first joined the police bureau, and we had sporadic contact over the years. I later learned that he had been the other detective with C.W. Jensen at the Newberg hostage situation in 1984. It seemed that things were coming around full circle.

In 1984, Kim Singer was working for KPTV and I agreed to appear on her Saturday night *Newsmakers*

program. This was an hour-long program dealing with
current community concerns, but I had concerns of my own.
First of all, my involvement with the task force was confi-
dential. I had always kept my police work as low key as
possible and sometimes as secret as possible. Since I rarely
appeared in court on cases, I could take a back seat to direct
involvement in specific cases we had profiled or investigated. I wanted to keep my part with the task force secret.
We did not know what we were up against and I did not
want to compromise the investigation by inadvertently
saying something inappropriate. No leads for the killer,
please. I was certain he was following the media closely.

In the case of the murdered boys, the public did
remain unaware of my part in the investigation until after
the arrest of Westley Allan Dodd. This was when the judge
released the profile outlining my involvement in the case
and pertinent details of my life and training. This, in itself,
was a new experience to me. Secondly, I was concerned
about the morbid aspects of the situation, and the ethics.
Some newscasters will play up the negative and horror-
tinged aspects of a murder or rape to appeal to certain
viewers. Kim Singer and I did discuss this prior to the
program I was on and fortunately she was professional in
every respect. If Portland were New York City or
Washington D.C., she would be at the top of her profession.
We agreed not to talk about the children's bodies, the
wounds and any horror tinged issues. This became especially important because, ironically, the program aired on
the evening of the Iseli boy's funeral! The program seemed
to help people put the situation in perspective and gave reas-
surance that the police were working hard on the case and
there was much concern. When the program was completed,
I commented to Kim Singer that I hoped the case would be

solved soon so I could get it over with and on to other things. Prophetically, she said: "Ron, this case will be with you for years and years and years."

Dodd, in the meantime, had carefully followed the news reports and learned about the formation of the task force of which I was a member. He took Lee's socks, shirt and other items of clothing and burned them in a trash barrel outside his apartment. He sliced up Lee's shoes, placed them in two sacks and attempted to burn them as well. As I had previously predicted in my psychological profile report, Dodd kept Lee's underwear and related items for "souvenirs."

Chapter 11

Standing Fast

—.—.——.—.—.——.—.——.——.——.——.—.—

Stand fast you Maine Boys.
          — Order given to Colonel Joshua L.
          Chamberlain and the 20th
          Maine on Little Round Top.
          Gettysburg 1864.

The dark figure appeared to be moving rapidly and I increased my pace, stepping carefully to secret my position. I continued casting furtive glances behind me. My right hand grasped the 9 millimeter semiautomatic carried in the small of my back. A habit — a sense of security. Had I remembered to put a round in the chamber? In a tight situation, seconds could mean the difference between life and death. The chief had once admonished me for keeping the chamber empty. I thought it was a safety measure — the chief thought it was dangerous. The figure made a quick turn and disappeared. I followed. Suddenly there was no one.

The same thing again. I bolted upright in bed, my heart pounding. Soon settling down, I kept the dream in mind to take up with Alex. Yes, my analyst. We would deal with the early developmental issues associated with security, danger and love. The need to "see" and to follow. To find. To overcome an obstacle. An enemy. To find the light. Of course, the obstacle, the enemy, was the faceless killer of trusting children. There was no doubt in the minds of the hunters that he would kill again.

The task force had spent time on about 160 suspects and I was sure one of them was our man. No such luck. A few false starts and many disappointments. Jensen and Trimble worked continuously. I wasn't always sure who else was totally involved, since police officers have many cases to work on at the same time. It's not like a television program where one case is followed through. There are many to keep track of, not enough time and not enough support personnel. The paper work involved in following leads is alone a major task.

I tried to imagine how the killer would re-appear. I started to drive by parks and playgrounds looking at the people standing around. Even during my park walks I made it a point to pass by the children's play area. Portland civic organizations have generously donated space and equipment for children including state-of-the-art safety swings and slides. There were a few more television programs dealing with parental concern but they were brief and anticlimactic compared to the *Newsmakers* program. The profile material was circulated to some police agencies in the area. My own life bumped along and I noticed the increased vigilance and less carefree approach to things. There is no compartmentalization of work when the intensity is at a peak.

On Saturday, November 11, Dodd went searching for another victim. He drove his 1974 Ford Pinto station wagon to a theater in Vancouver that he knew featured children's movies. He entered the theater, watched what was happening around him, and followed a seven- or eight-year-old child to the restroom. Inside, he grabbed the boy, who started yelling and screaming. Dodd struck the child. After punching the boy in the stomach to knock the wind out of him, he started to carry him out of the theater, pretending that the child was ill. Because the child yelled so much, Dodd decided to abandon the situation and ran out of the theater. He went home and masturbated.

The following evening, he went out again to the New Liberty Theater in Camas, a small town east of Vancouver. The movie playing was *Honey, I Shrunk the Kids.* Dodd knew there would be many children there. Because he arrived in time for the late show at 9:00 P.M., he decided to abandon the hunt at that point. I later obtained a copy of his diary, the diary we predicted would be in the possession of the killer when he was apprehended. His diary entries had been updated.

On November 13, he wrote:

> I now ask Satan to guide me, and provide or help me obtain a boy tonight. This one I'd like to keep awhile — keeping him awake all night each nite so he'll sleep all day while I'm at work (tied and mouth taped shut to be on the safe side). I may only keep him two or three days or even longer if it works out. I will give him a haircut and buy a new set of clothes for him, to change his appearance in case I take him out as I did Lee and number two. I might even get two boys ... in the case of two like this — the older (or both) will decide (when I'm tired of

them) which was to die.... I also want to do my medical experiments this time, once finished with sexual play on the body(ies). Also hoping for more, better pictures. May also play "spin the bottle" or stripping games, especially with two boys.

4:40 PM. Will now prepare ropes as I had to Incident #2, tied to bed and hidden under it — to use on victims as soon as wanted or needed — needing only to tie loose rope ends to the victim, other ends already attached to bed, or my "rack," my wood framework built for this purpose.

5:25 P.M. Now going to Camas - will check out local parks before a movie.

Dodd arrived at the New Liberty Theater. A young six-year-old had to go to the bathroom, passing by Dodd, who was watching the children who entered the theater. When the boy was exiting the rest room stall, Dodd stopped him. "I'm going to take you outside," he told the boy. The child resisted. Brazenly, Dodd picked the child up, put him over his shoulder and carried him out of the theater all the while punching him. By this time, the boy was screaming at the top of his lungs. Dodd ran out of the theater with the child, but in the meantime, someone called 9-1-1. As he turned the corner, Dodd disappeared, but he let the child go. The child returned terrified and crying to the co-owner of the theater. By this time, his mother's boyfriend, William Graves, obtained a quick description of Dodd and ran out of the theater. A short time later, he observed Dodd's Pinto stalled and Dodd cranking the engine trying to get it started. Graves pretended to help Dodd and they moved the car to a parking lot. At this point, Graves put Dodd into a hammerlock choke hold. The 1974 Ford Pinto station wagon, Washington license number 388CIUK remained in the lot. Police Officer Strong of the Camas Police Department made the arrest. The police report number 89-2310 was written by officers Strong, Norcross, Slyter and Chaney of the Camas Police Department. Men I knew.

The following morning, I received a telephone call about the arrest. Dodd was charged with kidnapping in the first degree. Was this our man? It was the beginning of the end.

The officers of the Camas Police Department stood their ground. Dodd did not pass through a bureaucratic crack. These officers did not bask in the glory of an arrest. They did not attempt to grandstand — no premature interrogation that could possibly disrupt the investigation. Instead, they notified the task force that this might be our man. Certainly a suspect. I believe there are heroes all around us, men and women and sometimes children who do what has to be done. People who put the welfare and greater good of others before their own. People who follow the path. John Keegan, the history writer, speaks of the need of hero leaders to wear a mask. A mask to which people-followers can project their hopes and needs. A hero in this sense embodies the unconscious aspirations of others. This is why I say that patriotism reflects the finest that a culture has to offer — the rising above national boundaries to a broader perspective. The heroes in our midst, however, do not need a mask. We all know who they are and when they are heroic. A few weeks ago, three firefighters in my city received the Medal of Valor for outstanding rescues. In an unrelated circumstance, one Portland citizen stood below the window of a burning building and caught the children as they jumped to safety. A nurse opened a free clinic in a run-down neighborhood to provide health care for the neglected — the castoffs.

It is very much to the credit of the officers of the Camas Police Department that they recognized the unusual nature of the kidnap situation and the possible murder connection. Officer R.L. Strong arrived on the scene and took statements from witnesses. He placed Dodd under arrest and notified Sergeant Don Chaney and Detective Doug Slyter, two well known veterans of the department. It was Detective Slyter who first fully interviewed the victim, James Kirk. James described in detail what had happened. Detective Slyter then ran Dodd's background through the NCIC (National Crime Information Center) and recognized that he had numerous prior charges of kidnapping, indecent exposure, lewd conduct and other offenses. In fact, there had been a recent attempted abduction in Seattle on June 13, 1987. These experienced officers put two and two together and realized that Dodd worked in close proximity to the game preserve and Vancouver Lake where Lee Iseli's body had been found. They also noted the proximity of Dodd's home address to David Douglas Park where Billy and Cole had been found murdered. They wisely decided to stand fast and not conduct an interview with Dodd, but to contact the task force.

This outstanding example of human concern and decency led to the full interrogation. Detective Dave Trimble of the Clark County Sheriff's Office along with Detective Rick Buckner were contacted and arrived at the Camas Police Department late in the evening, followed by C.W. Jensen from Portland.

Dodd was read his Miranda rights. He said he understood and signed the card. He was willing to answer questions without an attorney and openly discussed the incident that had occurred at Liberty Theater. Dodd was cagey about what he told the officers, however, omitting a great deal of his motivation and intent. He tried to focus the officers specifically to the Camas case, but they directed him to discuss his past arrests and difficulties. Jensen and Trimble did an outstanding job in not alienating Dodd and in drawing him out. In a sense, talking him down — deeper and deeper — in discussing a series of escapades involving live children and sadistic sexual fantasies. But fantasies are not acts. Dave Trimble introduced the issue of the homicides by asking Dodd if he was aware of what had occurred in the Vancouver area.

He caught Dodd off guard and he made an unconvincing comment about reading "something" in the newspapers. Dodd was fencing. It is not easy for normal human beings to sit in front of a potential serial child killer and maintain their composure. The urge is to jump up and shake the person and scream for a confession.

One such circumstance in Latin America resulted in a psychiatrist killing a person during an interview in which the individual confessed to multiple murders. But Jensen and Trimble stood fast and remained calm as they became convinced of Dodd's guilt. Jensen began pushing Dodd as to his whereabouts and personal behavior during the times the children were killed, establishing a chronology. He also wanted to examine Dodd's car and his house, but Dodd refused, indicating that he would have to think about this before granting the detectives permission. He did not, however, request an attorney. He thought he could handle the questioning by himself. After all, hadn't he done so numerous times before? Hadn't he pulled the wool over the eyes of judges dozens of times? Men of the law. Alleged experts. Now, the men confronting him were just small town cops. No big deal. Just another molestation charge. Maybe a few days in jail and a restitution fine. Plea bargain it down.

That night, Jensen and Trimble became heroes. The time had come. In police lingo, Dodd "broke" from relatively gentle but adroit and incisive questioning. Then, without emotion, as if teaching a class, he began to recount the murders to Detectives Jensen and Trimble. The information he gave was not complete as we were to learn later. But it was consistent with what the killer would later tell Detective Buckner and me — the gruesome details.

After having been notified of the arrest, I drove across the bridge to Vancouver and met with C.W. and Dave. They were disgusted with Dodd. Something so ugly — something so awful — perpetrated by someone like this! Standing in the stairwell of the jail, we reminded one another of the list of 160 suspects we had laboriously gone through. Some of these men had committed murder but Dodd's name was not among them. If there was any warmth or compassion in the story of the killings, it emanated from the officers themselves, especially Trimble and Jensen. They suffered every step of the way.

A short time later, I received a call from a fellow police officer in another department. He had heard the news of the arrest and blurted out that "the guy," meaning Dodd, must be "crazy." This comment upset me a great deal and I shot back that he wasn't. The officer was puzzled and thought maybe I was crazy. How could a sane person do something like this? I was in no mood to explain, but I worried about the jury jumping to the same conclusion and sending Dodd to a hospital for "treatment." There are numerous instances of killers released from hospitals, only to go out and kill again, and we've had our share in Oregon.

Roger Bennett, former Clark County Deputy Prosecutor and now Judge, District Attorney Art Curtis, Dave Trimble and I sat down to prepare an affidavit of probable cause for the issuance of a search warrant. Sitting in front of a computer, we highlighted what we knew and made history in Washington State. Included in the profile were significant parts of the psychological profile we had previously prepared. I was surprised that information regarding my background had to be included. A substantial portion of my résumé was made part of the affidavit and included was my science degree from Pennsylvania State University, medical degrees and medical-surgical training at the Bryn Mawr Hospital outside of Philadelphia. My psychiatric training at the University of North Carolina and the Oregon Health Sciences University was written in along with hospital appointments and a directorship of a private psychiatric hospital. Sixteen years of experience in homicide work was noted along with some other specific details, including mention of the profile I contributed in the I-5 killer case.

Our predictions set down in the current profile were reiterated and the similarities to our suspect were noted and highlighted for the judge. We even included our prediction regarding the use of restraints. Looking at the computer screen that day, it became obvious that we had described Westley Allan Dodd "to a T." We looked at one another impressed with our own accuracy. We knew what we had. Our profile set a precedent in Washington State in the production of the affidavit for a search warrant. The warrant was granted on the basis of the criminal profile we had structured!

Judge Robert Moilanen received the affidavit and signed warrants authorizing the searches of Dodd's apartment and his car.

Meanwhile Dave Simpson, the public information officer for the Portland Police Bureau, Dave Trimble, C.W.

Jensen and Art Curtis asked me to interrogate Dodd to gain
an enhanced perspective. I agreed, and Detective Buckner
asked if he could sit in. Little did I know that this pivotal
interview would be the cause for a suppression hearing
necessitating my testimony.

Chapter 12

The Dance

- — . — — . — — . — — . — — . — — . — — . — — . — — . — — . — —

O swaying music
O brightening glance,
Who can tell
The dancer from the dance
>   *— Yeats*
>   *King of the Great Clock Tower*

Bill Moyers has recounted one of Joseph Campbell's favorite stories about an American delegate, a social philosopher, at an international conference on religion in Japan. He was heard to say to a Shinto priest, "We've been now to a good many ceremonies and have seen quite a few of your shrines. But I don't get your ideology. I don't get your theology." The Japanese paused, as though in deep thought, and then slowly shook his head. "I think we don't have ideology," he said. "We don't have theology. We dance."

The dance we made with Westley Allan Dodd was a grim and macabre performance, particularly for us. As sensitive humans, Dodd was like a foul smell to us. A cunning aberration who killed for his pleasure, unmindful of the deep-seated black urge that dictated his homicidal forays for victims.

The concluding words of the search warrant issued by the judge allowing us to search the home of Dodd read:

"Based on the foregoing, I pray the court for the issuance of a search warrant. Respectfully submitted this 14th day of November, 1989."

I pray the court. I pray.

Rick Buckner wanted to sit in on my interview with Dodd. This was his first homicide case and he hadn't had much experience in this type of interrogation. Fortunately, after a false start we had a chance to talk and things worked out reasonably well. After all, I was on foreign turf. This was another agency in another city and *my* department was across the river and down the road. The interview was conducted in the Clark County jail. The people around were nice enough but the room was dreary and behind locked doors. The stone walls had been painted, perhaps centuries ago. Every so often, we were jarred by the loud sound of a buzzer as the jail matron let in a shackled prisoner or an attorney. We couldn't see this and no one could see us. Occasionally, during silent periods in the interrogation, we could hear the shackles scraping across the floor out near the entrance.

I had asked for a video camera but none was available, so Rick and I introduced ourselves to Dodd and asked him to sign the Miranda release. I flashed my badge and made it clear that I was a police officer. The issue of being a physician or psychiatrist never came up, although during the suppression hearing Dodd's attorneys attempted to say that I had misrepresented myself. Nothing was further from the truth. They also could not believe the accuracy of the profile and accused me of writing it *after* Dodd was apprehended. The judge believed me when I disagreed.

As is my custom, I began with a developmental history, asking questions about place and manner of birth, parental relationships, school experiences and so forth. Dodd was cooperative. About a half-hour into the interview someone knocked on the door and said he could procure a video camera but it would take about twenty minutes. I had second thoughts about stopping the flow at this point, but felt that the tape would be invaluable for courtroom use and so opted for this. Dodd agreed to be taped and we took a twenty-minute break during which time I chatted with Sheriff Kanakoa of Clark County and Chief Criminal Deputy, now sheriff, Gary Lucas. Gary was very helpful after the interrogation in terms of moral support and providing directions to the one crime scene and Dodd's apartment. In this catastrophe, everyone pulled together and I will be forever grateful for his acceptance and understanding. His reputation as a fine human being is well deserved.

After the interval, Buckner and I returned to the interrogation room and set up the camera. We read Dodd his Miranda rights while the tape was running and engaged in some preliminary talk. I was stunned when he told us how especially impressed he was with the *Oregonian* article about Lee Iseli. A mail lady had been interviewed and thought Lee was "special." Dodd thought Lee was special, too, and spoke of him in affectionate terms. He returned to the topic of the "mail lady" a few times. Long after this time, I wondered if perhaps no one ever thought of Dodd as special. Our videotaped interview lasted about three hours and the total procedure several hours more. I hadn't eaten all day, having rushed over from my office. It didn't matter. I offered Dodd some food, and he settled for a glass of milk. During the interrogation he elaborated quite definitively on the sexual assaults, mutilation and murder of the three boys. Perhaps he thought he would not be convicted without physical evidence. Perhaps he thought he could later change his story. I don't know. This was the confusing part, because he refused to allow us access to his car or apartment. What he didn't realize was that, at the very moment we were talking to him, the judge had authorized a search warrant on the basis of our psychological profile. The paper tiger became evidentiary material for the procurement of a search warrant, and the forensics teams were soon to be on their way to the apartment. This was a new experience for police in Washington State, but it worked, and while our interrogation proceeded, teams of experts took the apartment apart. The same was true for his automobile. Detective O'Toole and his two forensic technicians had plenty of work to do that night. They too made a video recording of Dodd's residence, inside and out. We knew the videos would be important but did not realize how important.

In interviewing homicide suspects, one must individualize. Not only is each perpetrator unique but there is a somewhat different style for purposes of a defense, prosecution or police interrogation. As criminals, serial murderers are in a category by themselves. A "psychology of evil" as Geberth would say. The strategy one uses in these interrogations must appeal to the serial killer's psychological makeup and self interest. These killers want to be "special" — important. They may even have subconsciously left clues that would lead to their apprehension. They view apprehension not as a form of punishment but as an opportunity for further aggrandizement. An increase in their self-importance results from the attention of news media, defense attorneys, judges and the public. They enjoy hurting the victims' families and some are openly brazen in courtroom scenes. These individuals also appreciate the shock value of their crimes and revel in their notoriety. Some openly display the bodies of their victims in provocative manner for further extension of their enjoyment.

Serial killers are also cunning and play a game with the interviewer. They deal well with the usual investigative techniques because they are detached both from the interviewer and the victims. Their emotional control is sometimes better than the interrogating officer's, who is repulsed and shocked. Any attempt on the part of the interrogator to evoke sympathy for the victims is a waste of time. These individuals are basically heartless, and one should anticipate multiple lengthy interviews. Establishing some kind of "relationship" with the suspect is important, and threats, criticisms or strong-arm tactics have no place in this setting. No Hollywood theatrics. No John Wayne comments. These individuals are and wish to be in control, and the more one can "ask" for their "help" the better. In this way, the serial killer furthers his own sense of importance, control and dominance over the police officers. The interrogator must not, however, kowtow to the suspect or grant all of his requests or demands. The presentation of authority, structure and kindness is important.

Candidness is extremely important. These individuals have followed the investigation and know more than you know and exactly what you know. Serial murderers have an interest in police investigative techniques, the legal system and forensics. They also have an idiosyncratic sense of logic. They know when you have incriminating information about them and it's acceptable to discuss this. The interrogating officer must have a thorough knowledge of the crimes that have been committed and a basic understanding of the psychopathology of personality disorders, especially of borderline and narcissistic states. Sometimes the killers recall better details about the crime than the interrogating officer. These individuals, who see themselves as being very important at this point in time, will try to gain legal advantages. This is one negotiating issue and represents a key to the personality of serial killers. They are working and living through their own egos. They wish to be important and cannot be belittled. In fact, it is helpful to comment regarding the suspect's abilities and intelligence, taking care to avoid patronizing him. These individuals are sadistic and are fascinated by the pain and suffering of others. They wish to shock everyone including the interrogator and can "get off on this," something that should be allowed since it brings forth volumes of information and confessional material. The killer wants to relive the events of his "work" and wallow in his sadistic acts and fantasies. This is the drive to talk about what he has done, and must be encouraged, especially by the detective's own curiosity. All personal feelings must be left outside of the interview — at least not expressed in any way through mannerisms, facial grimaces, body language or verbal comments. This calls for a seasoned interrogator able to handle the personal stress these interviews engender.

Buckner and I were both tired; the day was ending. We hadn't eaten anything since the night before, but food was out of the question now.

Dodd described his predatory behavior, consistent with material later found in his diary. This description was also consistent with the studies of neurologist Frank Elliott regarding the physical correlates of predatory behavior in humans. Dodd began looking for children on the Labor Day weekend and told us: "I thought of molesting, and I drove, and I saw the sign of David Douglas Park." He spent three hours at the park on Labor Day and describes seeing "... two boys at the bottom of the hill, in the wooded area near Andresen Road and the trail head. Their bikes were parked. One of them, Cole, was standing by the bikes." Buckner and I were hearing it first-hand. We looked at one another blankly. Dodd attracted Billy's attention and "... asked him to come with me ..." and Billy, the ten-year-old asked, "Why?" Dodd said, "I want you to do something for me. Bring your bikes." They then walked down from Andresen Road. Dodd asked their names and ages, and when they came upon some other boys he told Billy and Cole "not to talk to them."

When the trio reached the edge of the park, Dodd advised the boys to leave their bikes there and "... we walked to the bushes. I faced the boys and told them I wanted one of them to pull his pants down. Cole said, 'Why?' and Billy said 'Him,' meaning Cole. I got on my knees and I faced the trail to be sure to see if anyone was coming down the trail. I was on my knees and Cole pulled his pants down to his knees. He said, 'Why are you doing this?' I said, 'Because I have to do it. I'll let you go in a little bit.' "

"I leaned forward doing oral on him for four or five seconds and then I said, 'Pull your pants up.' "

Dodd thought that the children were about seven or eight years old and that Cole was the older one. He was not aware of their actual ages until watching the newscasts. He then said to Billy, "Okay, I want you to pull yours down now. He cried." Dodd then turned to Cole, "Okay Cole, pull yours down again." Both boys were on their knees and

Cole's back was to Dodd. "I pulled down my pants and my penis was out to put between his legs. To simulate intercourse. But I could not get an erection. I said, 'I'll let you go.' I had a six-inch fish filet knife. It was by my right leg in my sock under my pants. Billy was facing me and Cole was sideways. I stabbed Billy real quick and turned to Cole. I knew I could not let them go. They would identify me. I expected Billy to fall. I stabbed Cole and Billy ran off down the trail to Andresen. I stabbed Cole two or three times and I kept doing it. I got up to chase Billy because I didn't want him to get out on the road. I got him with my left hand and my knife was in my right hand. He spun around and said: 'I'm sorry.' He thought I was stabbing him because he wouldn't pull his pants down. I stabbed him a few times and then ran back up the trail to the park where the bikes were. I went back where Cole was to check the crime scene. To make sure I didn't drop anything that would identify me later. This took some time. I hadn't thought whether Cole pulled his pants up."

When he first looked at Cole's body, Dodd thought his "intestines were starting to come out" and at this point he realized the child's pants were still down and "it was his privates. I noticed that he was on his back totally to his left side with his eyes open and I checked the area and ran down the trail to the bikes. There was blood on my left hand and wrist and I put it in my pocket before I got to the trail. I put the knife back in the sheath. I knew I wanted to find a boy and molest him. So I took the knife to get them to come with me. To come with me or else. Then I wouldn't have to drag them along. I knew they would tell. When Cole pulled his pants down, I knew I wouldn't be able to let them go."

Buckner and I were able to establish that Dodd formulated the intent to kill at this point in time when Cole pulled his pants down. This would be important later — premeditated murder. An insanity defense was not likely to fly with this evidence. We cautiously elicited this type of material without putting words in Dodd's mouth.

After checking Cole and keeping his left hand in his pocket, Dodd passed a couple of older kids. Some young men were playing baseball and asked him to throw the ball back. He did not want to seem suspicious so "I kept one hand in my pocket" and threw the ball back. Later, when he was driving away, he heard sirens and "figured they had found the boys. I saw a heavyset guy running to the Minit-Mart." This was not a jogger but a man who was dressed in a coat. "I thought he saw the boys and was running for help."

Dodd's living situation involved a studio apartment which he had rented from an elderly woman who had a home in Vancouver. He paid $200 a month and had moved that Labor Day weekend. After killing Cole and Billy, he went home, took a shower and then visited his father. He returned home, and went to sleep. This wasn't easy because he was "scared." He worried that Billy might still be alive. There were no feelings of remorse or guilt. He had to report for work at 7:00 A.M.

"I actually killed him. I knew Cole was dead, but I wasn't sure about Billy. That's the first time I've ever killed anyone. I thought about it all day. They just found Billy."

Dodd followed the news very closely and thought that Cole had not yet been found. The children were not immediately identified.

At work the following day, Dodd was quiet, especially during lunch, and simply nodded his head when people talked. He was preoccupied. "I hope there were no witnesses there." He was concerned about some girls in the park and thought that they might have been pointing at him while telling stories. He worried that they might have identified him. "I figured they gave the artist the information for the drawing." Dodd told us that he had wrapped the knife up in a manila envelope, doubled the wrapping and put it in the garbage dumpster at work. He waited a day to do this because he had forgotten to do so the day after the murder. He said: "There was no way anyone could find it."

Dodd also considered that perhaps Billy had been alive long enough to identify him. "I heard that he was taken to the hospital and thought he could identify me. That had me scared. All week I thought about it quite a bit. I bought every edition of the *Oregonian* and the *Columbian* and other newspapers and, after a week, I thought I might get away with it. After a month, the fear went away and I started to want to molest a boy again. I knew I couldn't go back to David Douglas Park. I had a map of Portland and started looking for parks that were similar to David Douglas."

Dodd's initial concerns about the discovery of the children were justified. A 17-year-old came upon the body of Billy Neer and initially thought that the child may have been injured riding his bicycle or perhaps he had been hit by an automobile. At a nearby store, he telephoned 9-1-1 and Lieutenant Roy Brown, a patrol officer with the Vancouver Police Department, was the first to respond to the call. Paramedics were dispatched from a nearby fire station and they immediately recognized that the boy had been stabbed in the upper chest. There were also defensive wounds on his legs. There was still some hope that he might live and a Life Flight helicopter from Emanuel Hospital in nearby Portland was summoned. Emanuel Hospital is a trauma center for the area and especially significant because it specializes in the traumatic care of children. Joanne and I have a relative who is part of the Life Flight team and we also sponsored a trauma surgeon from China who worked on the program for two years. We have strong positive feelings about these wonderful rescuers from the sky.

The helicopter landed safely at Fort Vancouver High School and Billy was picked up and treated during the short flight to Portland. His injuries were extensive; he had lost a great deal of blood and was pronounced dead on arrival at 7:37 P.M. A deputy Oregon state medical examiner concurred that the child had died of stab wounds. No one could identify him however. There was no identification. That evening, Clair Neer telephoned the Vancouver police and reported Billy and Cole as missing. Jeff Sundby, a detective with the Vancouver department, began to wonder about an additional victim. Detective Sundby and his fellow police officers worked throughout the night. Eventually, the two children's bicycles were found near the trail. By 2:00 A.M., Cole was found dead at the scene. He had been stabbed in the chest and abdomen and there were defensive wounds on his extremities. Both boys were definitively identified.

Following the Neer murders, Dodd talked with his landlady, Vivian Shay. She later told authorities: "He told me he hoped they caught the man who did it. He seemed concerned about it." Vivian did not know much about Dodd nor did she notice anything suspicious about him. She described him as a person who "was real nice, real helpful. He paid his rent on time."

While Buckner and I listened to Dodd, we occasionally exchanged glances. It seemed as if our capacity to process experience was being pushed to the limit. Was this really happening? We were assaulted with an awful reality. As T.S. Eliot once wrote: "These fragments I have shored against my ruin...." Buckner and I had many times before studied the crime photos of the Neer boys. They were hard enough to take. Now we were putting reality to it. A reality that seemed in moments to be an illusion. We were indeed tired. What images would we ever use to erase the terrible pictures in our minds?

Dodd's confession was relentless. He said to us, referring to Cole Neer, "I thought I got away with it. I wanted to spend more time with the kid. I thought I'd want to get a kid home and have him for the weekend. After work, I went over to see what the park looked like. I checked it out. I wanted to see it during the day. Saturday night when I was going home up Division Street, I saw a school building. It was dark and there were a lot of kids around the school."

Dodd was exhibiting typical pedophilic behavior without coaxing from us. He was looking for "double victims." Such youngsters are frequently the children of broken homes or children previously molested. Sometimes they are children who are simply neglected or abandoned. Pedophiles have a radar sensitivity for their victims. Their ability in this respect is uncanny. Dodd passed up one potential victim about six or seven years of age because he thought there were a number of people around doing "drug deals. This wasn't the place."

On Sunday morning, he drove to David Douglas Park once again, looked for and found the school and began cruising. He saw some children playing near the volcano — the mound. There was a small boy on top and three others, two of whom were playing football. Dodd drove to the opposite side of the building so he wouldn't be seen and parked his car opposite the school and opposite the volcano. He walked around the end of the building.

"I got out of the car and went around the block," he said. The older boy was with his brother. At first, Dodd thought this might be an adult, but then realized he was a child. The third boy was watching the two others play football. Dodd went up to the small child and said: "Hi, how would you like to make some money playing games? ... Neat games. It would be a lot of fun." He reached his hand out. The child's brother, in the meantime, turned to watch the football game.

At this point in our interrogation-interview, Dodd began talking baby talk! Buckner and I were spellbound. A pedophile in action. He spoke to the child and to us in baby talk demonstrating how he lured small children to his side. I was stunned. One professor calls this behavior "malignant pseudo-identification." Dodd advised the child to get into the car and told him: "We will go and ask your dad if it's okay for you to come with me and play games."

It was that easy. They drove off and he told Lee: "We are going to my house." At this point, the Iseli child "almost started to cry, but I said we'll go play games and this is your chance to make some money. I got him calmed down. About half way to my home, he wanted to go back and not to my house. He wanted to be with his brother. He thought his brother might miss him and he said so, and I said he won't miss you, he's having fun too. He was scared about staying with me. I carried him out of the car and he said he could walk. So he walked with me and we went to the back of the house and we went in. He was uneasy and he didn't want to go in. I said we'll just play a few games and I'd take him home. We went into the house and I took a Polaroid camera and took a picture of him with his clothes on and showed him my photo album with other pictures. I have pictures in my book from *National Geographic* of children without any clothes on and I told him I always take pictures of kids. I showed him the pictures and then said 'now take your clothes off.' He was on the bed."

Once again at this point in the interview, Dodd lapsed into baby talk. "You have to," meaning take his clothes off. "I'll take pictures of you like the other pictures. I pulled his shoe off and he pulled his own pants and underwear off. He was on his back and I took a picture of him on his back and a picture on his stomach and I asked him if it was okay if I touched it. I'll put my mouth on it now. I had pictures of myself without clothes, but with an erection and I asked him if he remembered me with it up. I told him I wanted a picture of him with it straight up. He needed oral so I did oral, but he didn't get an erection. Other boys would get an erection when I did it. I said okay. I have ropes on my bed frame. They were already there, but they were hidden out of sight. I told him I wanted to tie him up. I put a robe on him between pictures, tied the ropes to his wrists and ankles and waist. He was spread eagle. He laid with his hands behind his head. Maybe he didn't think it was all that bad. I just wanted a picture of him tied up and I told him I would let him go. I did take the picture that I wanted."

Buckner and I now understood the ligature marks on Lee Iseli's body. After this scenario, Dodd put the ropes in the garbage and later retrieved them. Eventually, he burned them and purchased new ones for his next victim. He purchased the same type of rope — a cotton clothesline type. We would later correlate this information with what the forensic team found in Dodd's residence. Dodd continued with his unhesitating account:

"I let him get under the covers of the bed. I'll teach you how adults make love. I kissed him a few times and he kissed me and I took my clothes off in bed and got under the sheets and moved to simulate intercourse. I put him on his stomach and put my penis between his legs and had him on his back again. I told him some white stuff would come out. He said okay and I ejaculated on him. I cleaned him up and cleaned myself up and gave him his clothes and he had trouble getting dressed and put his shirt on first."

After this, according to Dodd, he and the boy watched cartoons for a few hours. Dodd said a Walt Disney special was on and that the boy was in a good mood and less frightened. At this point, Dodd estimated that the child was about four or five years of age. Lee wanted to draw and Dodd gave him paper and a pencil. He drew, but then decided that he wanted to go home and Dodd told him: "Not just yet. I'm sorry we don't have any toys and he said that's okay. I said let's go to K-Mart and buy you a toy and then we'll go to McDonald's for dinner and you can spend the night with me. I told you you'd have fun."

While Dodd detained and exploited Lee, a man named Ken came to visit. Lee wanted to give Ken a picture and Ken assumed that the child was Dodd's nephew, a fabrication Dodd was only too happy to perpetuate. "He wants to give you a picture, Ken." Ken accepted the picture and left after a very brief time.

They went to K-Mart and by this time it was about 6:00 P.M. They bought a toy called a "He Man," then went to McDonald's across from the K-mart. Dodd tried to keep Lee "in a good mood." After parking the car, they went in for a cheeseburger and after eating, played on the swings outside the McDonald's. After insisting to Lee four times that they would have to go back to the house, the duo left.

Once home, Dodd put on a pot of coffee and Lee began drawing again. Lee upset the coffee and spilled some on his shirt. Because it was hot, Dodd told him to take his shirt off. Lee hesitated but then pulled it off and Dodd noticed the red spot on Lee's chest.

He began nurturing the child, first by putting him on the bed and then putting a cold cloth on it. Dodd also gave Lee one of his T-shirts to wear. He asked Lee to spend the night with him and promised they would go to McDonald's again tomorrow. The child drew more pictures, watched television and then wanted to read books. He wanted to put the pictures that Dodd had taken of him into the picture book where the other children were. He did put his pictures in, but later Dodd took them out because he considered his album to be "art."

By this time it was about 8:30 P.M. and time to get ready for bed, but they stayed up until about 10:30. Lee told Dodd that he was used to staying up late. Dodd asked the child to sleep with him and told us that Lee consented. Dodd told Lee he always slept in his underwear, but he wanted the child to sleep with as little as possible on. The child was asleep within five minutes; and, at this point, said Dodd, "I pulled his clothes off. I did oral on him during the night several times. I put my penis between his legs and held it there. He woke up coughing. I sat him up and then I laid him back down. I would occasionally do oral on him. He woke up and I asked if it was okay to leave his pants off. He was tired and said it was okay."

At this point it was about 3:30 in the morning and Dodd described his intent to kill the child. This portion of his confession was important because it established premeditation.

"I pulled him on me for half an hour and he woke up. I started to think. I need to get ready for work. What am I going to do? He woke up and I said I'm going to kill you in the morning. He said, 'No you're not,' and he seemed scared."

Buckner and I furtively glanced at one another. I cannot explain the feelings I experienced listening to this.

By this time it was 4:00 A.M.. Dodd soothed the boy by saying, " 'I'm kidding.' But then I thought how to do it."

At 5:30 A.M., he thought and said: " I knew I could not miss work. He was on his back and I was on my left side facing him. He was a nice kid and I hated to do it, but I had to. His hands were lying on his sides." Dodd described how he put his leg over the child and held him down. He choked him with one hand, while Lee struggled and twisted on the bed. The child began kicking his feet to move away and did a quarter circle on the bed. At this point, Dodd employed both hands to strangle Lee. He realized the child was dead at this point and then decided to do CPR on a mouth-to-mouth basis just to see what would happen. He was omnipotent — killing and bringing back to life.

The child started breathing again and gasping. Dodd took the rope attached to the bed and placed it around Lee's neck. "I pulled it tight," he said. "I pulled it into a loop and I held him for awhile. I wanted to hold him as he was dying. I held the rope tight and I carried him over to the closet. I hooked him up in the closet. I took a picture of him hanging in the closet."

Dodd used the Polaroid. He said that the child's chest heaved.

"He kept fighting. He wanted to live. I went to brush my teeth in the bathroom and I was getting ready for work. I then put the body on the shelf in my closet. It's a narrow closet and I put him on the top shelf. I put his knees up and one arm around his belly and blankets over it." Dodd was concerned that the landlady might look in the closet, but he thought probably she wouldn't; but even if she did, the child would be covered. He piled a yellow and white and a blue blanket over the body, as well as a sleeping bag. Then he went to work.

"I tried to act as normal as possible," he said. He told us it was Monday, a hectic day and he was "very busy. I missed lunch and both breaks."

Dodd went home at 4 P.M. Monday afternoon, took the body out of the closet and put it on the bed. He noticed it was stiff and cold. The skin was purple. Dodd spread the child's legs apart, took pictures of him on the bed and then laid him on his stomach. He then put on a condom and had anal intercourse with the child. He thought it would be cleaner with a condom. "I didn't want to get so dirty." At this point, he cleaned up, left the dead child on the bed and went out to purchase some garbage sacks. Returning, Dodd put Lee's body in the sacks and carried him outside where he placed him on the passenger side of his car. It was about 7:30 P.M.

Dodd drove to Vancouver Lake and down a road, which he realized was a dead end. He figured no one was around so he left the headlights on and dropped the body out of the bag leaving it exposed. He was able to see the abandoned child in his headlights. He left Lee like a pile of garbage, returned home, threw the bags away and put the photographs — his trophies — in his briefcase. He kept a diary of these events. He placed the child's underwear in his briefcase, but burned the outer clothes in the barrel outside the house. The retained underwear, was, he said, "for a souvenir, I guess." He also had news clippings of the murder of the Neer boys.

At this point in the interview, Dodd spoke again about the article in the *Oregonian* known as "Rest Easy." He was particularly moved by this piece since the "mail-lady" characterized Lee as a "special child." Nevertheless he said: "I tried to get back to life as usual." The following night, he burned Lee's shoes and continued to follow the investigation in the newspapers.

"I thought I'd get away with it. It was on the news." It was then he realized that: "They thought Lee was picked up on a street corner. It looked like I was gonna get away with it. I thought about molesting again."

What this meant to Dodd was that no one actually saw him at the playground. Free of anxiety of being caught, he formulated plans to attend movie theaters in Camas, where children gathered to eat popcorn and gaze at the screen full of imaginary heroes and villains.

Chapter 13

The Abyss

And when you look long into an abyss,
The abyss also looks into you.
        – Nietzsche
        Beyond Good and Evil

Nietzsche's statement above certainly expressed the revulsion Buckner and I felt for Dodd. Both of us felt that we had been tainted by a depravity so deep that it must have a dimension other than human. But we had no choice except to continue. We were learning a great deal about him and preparing for his prosecution.

My personal life was unsettled. Joanne's independence and quietness were getting on my nerves. The analysis was driving me nuts and I seemed to be the bad guy. I wanted more nurturing from Joanne but didn't realize I was not giving any. I guess I was away. Perhaps I was reflecting some of the taint from Dodd. It was true that I felt unclean. But Joanne seemed to withdraw the more I demanded attention. Rilke once wrote: "I was in ignorance before the heavens of my life." This about summed up my position in the days following Dodd's arrest. I developed a variety of psychosomatic problems. I, who had never been ill, developed pneumonia and had to undergo a heavy course of antibiotics. Then I was stung by a bee and developed cellulitis, which became toxic and caused me some mental confusion. Two doctors helped with this problem. My arm was as swollen as a cadaver and reminded me of the putrefying arm of a dead woman I'd once seen in the woods. I couldn't work for a week because my arm had to be continuously elevated. My brother died of cardiovascular disease and one of my long-term patients was killed by a gunshot wound. I was miserable about my patient and punished myself somewhat. As a memorial to her, I wrote and published a paper about her courage. My brother and I were separated by time and age and his loss was somewhat less painful, but everything seemed to be falling apart. Still, my grieving was intellectual. After a very minor fall, I injured my back and developed a foot drop — a neurological condition which caused me to drag the foot when walking. The doctors were equivocal about surgery so I waited and used a cane. I lost the reflexes in my right leg and treatment with anti-inflammatories and muscle relaxants only made me tired. My spinal column was not holding up and all of this pain only made me feel worse psychologically. Thank God I was back in therapy! I had lost my center and my confidence but I still maintained an intellectual belief in the power of life and psychiatry. I just knew things would, or at least could, get better. I gave up all extraneous physical and recreational activities and just worked and existed. I found myself tearful at the slightest comment. It was even painful to lie on the analytic couch during therapy sessions but I knew this was my only hope. The term that came to my mind that best described my condition, was Jelly Belly.

Things would get better. Once, after a session with Alex, my car stuck in the mud and his next patient came out to help me. I was morbidly embarrassed. In my therapy sessions, I attacked Alex for what I perceived to be mistakes of one kind or another. He guided me through this and I dealt with the misperceptions of my childhood and adult life. These confrontations in analysis were not easy. Therapy is hard work and can be exhausting. I tested and corrected my perceptions. My dreams were still filled with comings and goings. I wasn't even aware of the vulnerabilities of my emotional state. Dave Bishop's vulnerability was in viewing bodies of young women and the equation with his own daughters. The same process was operative with other police officers in the Dodd case. They, in their own ways, were drawn into the blackness of Dodd's twisted soul and had been touched and changed by its evil. My focus was the devastating loss of my father and the recapitulation of the grief issues associated with it. The children in the Dodd case were a factor, but the connection with my early parent loss was the main issue. My over-developed sense of responsibility, guilt and mastery–control issues were interwoven with my sadness. Even my father's strangulation from cancer replicated the dream images associated with Lee Iseli's death. They were later to replicate with another major theme. Alex, ever faithful, encouraged me to free-associate over episodes from my life and my dreams. In one dream a young man is being prepared for a casket in my childhood home. I couldn't bear to watch it; it seemed huge, very cold and very high off the ground. In the dream, I was furious — it was horrible to expose a child to such a scene. In a fashion, the dream made me think of my father's death.

Pop died at home and was laid out on the bed before he was embalmed. His body was placed in a huge casket that remained in our living room for days before the funeral. I was afraid to walk through the room, especially alone. The casket was so heavy and there were so many mourners that the living room floor had to be reinforced from below. Mom sat beside the casket, dressed in black. The room was full of candles, all night long for nights and nights. To a ten-year-old, this solemn scene was frightful, and I could barely see inside when Pop's pipe and glasses were put inside. The dream signified a desire to join him.

So many years later this loss was still an issue rekindled by the murder of three children. It is impossible to mourn the loss of a parent who dies before a surviving child's adolescence is worked through. I was no different. A child internalizes responsibility for the parent's death and carries the guilt indefinitely. This was a childhood problem because there was no one to trust and talk to, and I ran from the feelings and emotional impact. The only emotion I recall is how proud I was of the number of mourners who were at Pop's funeral. Also, that black people attended in a time of segregation. My father was a fair and honorable man, respected by all. I was so embarrassed about his death that I never told anyone at school what happened. Not even my teachers. It was school — business — as usual. The shadow followed me.

As early as 1963, my dream journal reflected my emotional sandbagging. I dreamt of Hamlet and being in the play, only I have no emotion and believe, therefore, that I'm doing a terrible job of acting. The theatrical metaphor was that there was something I wanted to create and feel — to feel. To be genuine. I presented a mask to the world. These issues were, however, becoming quickly resolved, especially the second time around in analysis. The unconscious dynamics and destructive tendencies were becoming conscious and a more complete resolution of my Oedipal difficulties was occurring. As a result, I became more comfortable with success of all kinds and developed a better take-charge style. This was to happen later, and in the meantime, my changes were not happening fast enough to suit Joanne. She had grown tired of me, my eccentricities, boredom, obsessions and narcissism. I had become a solipsist.

Finally, she could take no more. Shortly before we were to take a trip to Seattle, where I was to give a lecture, she announced she was leaving! She would still help in the office. No problem with the checkbook. She wasn't cleaning me out financially. She just wanted to leave. She said that while I was in Seattle, she would pack up some of her belongings and be gone by the time I returned. But where? After thirty years of marriage, where would she go? Certainly the warning signs had been there. Her announcement knocked me for a loop. I was still using the cane and taking medicine and I wasn't sure I could drive to Seattle alone. My requests fell on deaf ears. No matter, she was leaving.

During World War II, the United States stationed one million soldiers in the Aleutian Island chain to prevent an anticipated Japanese invasion. This became known as "the thousand mile war" because of the distance of the islands along the chain. Some heavy fighting did occur, and this was the only place the Japanese gained a foothold on American soil. The U.S. took heavy casualties in some battles and some of the Japanese, in deference to the Emperor, committed suicide. When the American soldiers gained the upper hand, the Japanese navy and troops were able to escape under cover of heavy fog and rough seas. The area has remained an important strategic post, especially for monitoring ship movements and communications. There is also a Long Range Aid to Navigation (LORAN) station there. In 1970, while I was in the military, I was dispatched to the Navy TDY (temporary duty) and sent to Adak Island far out in the chain. This proved a difficult assignment. After a day's flight in uncomfortable military transport, I was exhausted and looked for a place to sleep. Not fully familiar with navy protocol, I bunked down in the nearest quarters available. It was late at night, dark, and no one was around. Finding a bunk, I quickly fell asleep. A deep, restful sleep. When I awoke in the morning, I thought I recognized a familiar piece of clothing on the person in the next bunk. Silk and pink at that. I soon discovered that the individuals on each side of my bunk were navy nurses! That wasn't the difficult part. The navy soon transferred me to a smaller and more remote island. Both on Adak and on the smaller island there were still extensive minefields. Occasionally, one would explode as time wore away the detonating mechanisms. There wasn't much "to do" there and the beaches were obviously off limits. I began to miss Joanne's touch, not specifically sex but the actual body to body contact. The hugging and skin contact. I felt sensory-deprived and remember thinking of Sisyphus and his stone. And here I was many years later, in the aftermath of the Dodd investigation and Joanne's departure, feeling the same way!

Joanne has always helped me in the office and pursued her own interests, especially regarding abused and neglected children lost in the court system, and children who were without a permanent home. She continued with both, and I trudged on. Not wanting to have much contact with me, she did most of the book work that needed to be done, and other tasks, outside the office, or came in when she knew I was in session with a patient. She would also leave a note on my desk at home when communication was needed. I would respond with a note. She would arrive at the house after I left in the morning. Joanne took an apartment at the Quintet Apartments, ironically a stone's throw from Sunset Cemetery. This apartment complex is guarded like Fort Knox and no errant husband can find his way in. She also purchased an answering machine with a robotic voice. I both hated and admired the machine. I was taken aback the first time I heard this impersonal response. How I came to look for her notes! Going home to a partially empty house was spooky. The bedroom was absent her bureau and books. Her robe wasn't draped over the chair anymore and there were no loafers or slippers around the closets. Dreary! I rarely made the bed, so the place became a bit of a mess, and I had to arrange washing clothes in the evenings while I prepared a second-rate dinner or followed up on clerical tasks. Although I'm a great critic, cooking is not my forte. I also noticed that some of our special items were gone, like the small ebony elephant we bought in Africa and the colorful dolphin tiles we had in the kitchen to brighten up the counter. Characteristically, I was left with the bust of Lenin, purchased in Russia many years before.

Eventually, I did get to visit her apartment. I loved it! There was a balcony and three other rooms. The communication system with the office and gate keepers was excellent, and mobility throughout the complex was easy and elegant. I discovered that some tenants had purchased comfortable condominiums there, and Joanne made a comment about this being a possibility for her. In another, well secluded section, she showed me an Olympic sized swimming pool, Jacuzzi and excellent, clean exercise facilities. I tried to talk her into coming back. I was covetous of her living situation even though I had the house, and she didn't seem to need me to be complete. I thought of what the feminists say: "A woman needs a man like a fish needs a bicycle."

On rare occasions, we met for a very early breakfast or lunch. Mostly to talk about bills or arrangements for house repair, pest control, the garden and the mundane issues that occupy a family. But we were no longer a family — no longer a couple. Joanne liked Papa Haydn's restaurant, well known for its excellent desserts. I don't eat desserts and this wasn't my favorite place, but I acquiesced whenever she agreed to lunch. One night we met at the Heathman Hotel bar for a glass of wine, and I thought of the good times we'd had there. There were also some bad times, and I was embarrassed thinking of them.

Her island was genuine but not broad. She seemed happy but not effusive. I couldn't "read" her. I was a psychiatrist with past training in clandestine arts and I couldn't understand my own wife! I turned to Dave Bishop for some advice and he was always reassuring. "Don't do anything stupid. Just wait," were his comments. With the back pain, sleep problems, self-criticism intensified by the introspection of analysis, and alienation from friends who took Joanne's "side," I became a textbook case of delayed stress reaction. One of Joanne's friends told her: "Take the money and run." It was the end of the ninth and the score was not in my favor. It was interesting that Dave Bishop still felt I could handle police duties and he never asked for my gun or badge. No fitness for duty examination. He knew I was doing what I could. He had seen me under fire before and knew I had to work this out myself. There was no need to further undermine my confidence.

My patients seemed to do well, although I minimized the load as much as possible and also referred dangerously disturbed patients to others. Interestingly, I had been the one to take the difficult cases in years past. Even my analyst knew that I could handle tough problems and referred patients to me. Not now though.

One day, our family lawyer called and said he heard we were getting divorced. I was furious and told him this was nonsense. He was cagey and would not tell me where he had heard the rumor. Dave Bishop was more of a friend. On November 15 he sent me a letter:

> *Ron,*
> *I wanted to take this opportunity to congratu-*
> *late you on your assistance in solving the Iseli and*
> *Neer brothers murders. I am very proud of what*
> *you accomplished.*
> *You are to be commended for a job well done.*
> *Congratulations!!*
> *Sincerely,*
> *David G. Bishop*
> *Chief of Police*

Bishop's note really boosted my morale. At least I had done something right and we were learning more about Dodd and finding that our assumptions — our hypotheses — were correct.

At the time I met Westley Allan Dodd, he was 28 years of age. Born in Toppenish, Washington, he grew up "everywhere" in Washington State. His father worked for a dairy doing door to door deliveries and his mother, a woman in her late forties, remained a homemaker. He did not find love in the family and was disappointed with the parenting he received, especially his mother screaming: "I hate you, I hate you," when she sent Dodd to his room for punishment. His parents divorced when he was in junior high school, a situation that resulted in a sense of relief for Dodd as he described his parents as constantly arguing, even on vacations and camping trips. He denied any overt expressions of affection in the family, and told us that his two younger siblings were favored by the parents and they bonded, excluding Dodd. Dodd withdrew after the birth of his brother 11 months younger and his father described him as becoming a loner even at such an early age. Something had gone awry during the separation-individuation phase. Frequent relocations disrupted the establishment of close friendships with other children and Dodd never had a "best buddy." He found himself isolated from family members and friends. He was always embarrassed about changing clothes or taking showers at school, and referred to humiliation at home in matters pertaining to his body. He never dated during adolescence, even though he had an interest in music and some talent. His first homosexual experiences began at the age of eight and continued in the form of public exposure. He practiced flashing at students walking past his house by exhibiting his genitals from an upstairs window. He reported no positive feelings about the opposite sex and was teased by girls at school. He denied the usual heterosexual fantasies of men and boys. By junior high school years, his episodes of exposure from his upstairs bedroom continued until a policeman called on him. After the divorce when Dodd was 13, his mother married a violent alcoholic who almost killed Dodd's sister. This further drove Dodd out of the household, and when his father married a women with two children, Wesley began molesting the eight-year-old on a regular basis, until they moved away. What was described by Dodd was an existence devoid of any love or affection, and a turning towards physical–homosexual outlets. He was under investigation for public exposure while in high school and missed a band trip, but was proud that he helped the police "clear some files" at that time — his own.

This experience began a series of charges being filed and eventual mental health counseling. There were repetitive confrontations with small children and the authorities, but Dodd evaded the system. In a sense, he was aided and abetted by his parents, counselors and the courts. This was not always the case, and at least one astute case worker recognized Dodd's homicide potential. Judges turned away from firm decisions. As Dodd told us: "I could have been stopped over ten years ago but, each of those times, no charges were filed. By the time I graduated from high school, I had been caught five times and reported to police only three times." He learned to outsmart the police but was no match for Jensen and Trimble. Some counseling was destructive. One counselor instructed him on "what guys could do together. Different positions." His preference was for children eight or nine years old and medium build, especially blond boys with their hair parted in the middle. He developed a game of taping a coin on the body and having to search for it blindfolded. Finally, after graduation from high school, Dodd was charged with communication with a minor for immoral purposes. There were several children involved, and he joined the U.S. Navy in 1981 to have the charges dropped.

In the navy, Dodd continued his pedophilic activities offering children money in exchange for sex. Eventually, two boys reported him and he was given a general discharge "for the good of the U. S. Navy." He was relieved to leave.

After the navy, Dodd moved to western Idaho, took a temporary job and resumed his molesting activity. He described a long series of sexual encounters with children, as many as 80 by the time he was arrested in Camas. Once, he was given a one-year sentence and served four months. He moved back to Washington and did babysitting to molest children. Eventually, he moved from the Tri-Cities area when people began to suspect his activities. In Seattle, he was arrested by a security guard after attempting to kidnap a seven-year-old boy. He plea bargained the charge down to "attempted indecent liberties" and the judge further reduced the charges to "attempted unlawful detainment." He was given a counselor, but lost interest. He later had one heterosexual encounter — the only time in his life. He had intercourse with a woman, standing up in a hallway. However he noted his preference: "But, ah, anyway I kept molesting her son and I ended up getting out of there." Eventually, Dodd took a vacation with his father and step-mother and moved to Vancouver, finding a job with Pack Paper Company through a temporary service. Within a short time, he had enough to rent his studio apartment, moving in over Labor Day, and deciding to "go out for a while and begin molesting boys again … I decided I was going to go out and find one … I saw a sign that said David Douglas Park.…"

After Buckner and I finished the interrogation, we were both exhausted. I talked to Gary Lucas for awhile and we both thought it was a good idea for me to get over to Dodd's studio apartment. It was 2 A.M. I drove alone and parked up the street. After all, as far as the public knew, I was still a background player in this scenario. What I saw amazed me. As I walked down the street, the scene was surrealistic. News teams had set up massive lights on each side of the street. There were also large beacons that reminded me of a movie set. The news people had no idea that I had just left Dodd and I moved quietly and nonchalantly down the street toward the apartment. A nobody. I did not want to talk to anyone, let alone newspeople. My nerves were raw. Once at the apartment, I noticed it was compulsively neat and clean. The forensic team had already found the belts and ropes and there was also a set of knives. The bed had been dismantled, and strands of rope were attached to each corner. I thought of a horror movie! This was real. Everything was photographed and videotaped. An undeveloped roll of 35-millimeter film was taken and Dodd's "torture rack" and his diary were still in open view. On a side table was a copy of the New Testament. I felt vindicated — the materials we predicted they would find were there. The team performed vacuum sweepings of the rug before removal and not a stone was left unturned nor a fiber left unexamined. The apartment and Dodd's Pinto were processed for fingerprints.

As we had predicted, inside Dodd's briefcase was a pair of boy's underpants with the inscription "Real Ghost Busters" — one of Dodd's "trophies." These objects are used to relive the murder and sex through masturbatory fantasy, sometimes to the point of frenzy. There were a variety of handwritten documents which made up Dodd's diary, substantially organized and labeled as incidents one, two, three, etc. The news clippings were also in place. Every aspect of this situation included the use of these items to relive his experiences consistent with material noted in his journal. He had also taken photographs of himself involved in sexual acts with Lee Iseli ante and post mortem. Nude photos were present showing Dodd in a sexually aroused state. There were other photographs of Lee's body taken after the child was dead. One photo showed him hanging from a rope inside Dodd's closet. There was an additional notation in the diary dated Thursday, November 4 describing how Dodd would tie up a child, use a plastic bag and suffocate him. He had already gone to the lumber store, purchased wood and constructed his "torture rack." Driving home that night, I thought I might get lost. I felt confused. I thought that I could never tell a soul about this. No one would believe it!

The fact is, while most people are horrified when a monster like Dodd is revealed, they don't relate his appearance to the condition of the society that cultured him. Let me make this vague implication clearer by saying that, during his correspondence with Albert Einstein, Sigmund Freud commented to the famous physicist that "whatever fosters the growth of civilization works at the same time against war." Freud was equally direct when discussing the "essentials of violence" and how destructive impulses are facilitated by rationalization and dehumanization.

Of course, serial killers are the worst examples of human beings who, in the true sense of the expression, "kill in cold blood." These are people who have never developed the empathetic capacity for understanding or feeling the pain of others. They are people who can never be treated or repaired because, like the person who is born without an eye or limb, there is no replacement, no cure for an organ that does not exist — for a human who is devoid of humanity.

Lacking normal feelings, the serial killer is motivated by a deep rage whose origin lies in an overpowering hatred of his mother — his "bad" mother whom the killer has psychologically split off from the "good" mother.

It is usually the bad mother the serial killer continues to murder in the person of a chosen individual (the victim) who has been dehumanized in the killer's mind. In a sense, by torturing and slaying the victim, the killer is controlling "the badness" inside himself. Of course, he can never eliminate the badness, but he continues to try with one victim after another.

In his book *Civilization and Its Discontents,* Freud studies the primitive nature of man and, no doubt, would view the destruction of children as antithetical to life and an act in the service of the "death instinct." Man has not risen as far as he thinks and his unconscious represents chaos and aggression. We live behind a thin veneer of civilization. We are never far from the chaos and aggression, and I foresee an increase in the destructive tendencies of man resulting in human pain and loss, as societal and individual boundaries are broken. The disintegration of the family structure and de-emphasis of religious and moral values has left a deep vacuum and loosened the civilized controls of people. The vacuum has created a deficit in the internalization of values — a loss of conscience, and a loss of our humanity.

The resulting destructiveness remains elusive and hidden from easy detection, with the product of deterioration all too obvious.

Mind is more than an outgrowth of rational processes and it is difficult, even painful, to realize that the increasing aggression, of which we are reminded too often by shocking headlines in our newspapers, is determined by irrational forces. This is one explanation of the death instinct. I am not a doomsayer, but unless we rebuild the solid core of family unity that once gave strong morality, love and deep purpose to our nation, we are going to create more feelingless monsters who kill randomly and remind us by their increasing presence that the fabric of our lives is being torn asunder because we have abandoned that which made our lives worthwhile and virtuous.

Eastern religious thought, psychoanalysis and Native American perspectives teach us about the smoldering, unconscious drives that lie just beneath the surface of our civility and about their potential destructiveness. Religions as diverse as Buddhism and Christianity teach love and concern for the other as well as the self. Judaism gave the world morality. These values, however, are taught in the family home. This non-self centered subjectivity provides a sense of unity and timelessness. In contrast, the function of hatred provides an "other" to compare ourselves to and the hatred in the self is projected to others. This is the under-lying psychological process of the serial killer.

In his paper, "The Taboo of Virginity," Freud discusses how each individual is separated from others by a "taboo of personal isolation," and he applied the term "narcissism of minor differences" to differences in people who are otherwise alike. This narcissism forms the basis of hostility and strangeness which opposes the feelings of fellowship, thereby overwhelming the commandment that all men should love one another. Every intimate relationship leaves a sedimentary feeling of aversion and hostility, and repres-sion is used to control and hide these feelings.

Vamik Volkan, who wrote *The Need for Enemies and Allies,* observed that human beings use and need enemies as external stabilizers of their own sense of identity and inner control. We displace to others our aggression and establish an "other." In this same vein, Anna Freud noted that aggres-sive acts are preceded in the aggressor by a withdrawal of the feeling of sameness, thus facilitating the dehumaniza-tion process. This is the dynamic of serial killers. It also describes the accelerated process of depersonalization in our society, one of the consequences of family disintegration that leads to more violence and loss of faith in the ideals and morals that in the past have prescribed the ethical conduct of our nation and its citizens.

It is never enough merely to describe a social phenomenon such as serial killers when their number and the frequency of their appearances seem to be rising. And when we see symptomatic examples of their sociopathic behavior in less violent individuals, who, nevertheless exhibit the aggressive signs of displacement, rationalization and depersonalization, we must conclude that there is a growing sickness in our society with which we must deal.

Chapter 14

A Walk In the Sun

— · — · — · — · — · — · — · — · — · — · — · — · — · —

*I have a strong romantic fantasy about things
— and that's what I paint, but I come to it through
realism. If you don't back up your dreams with
truth, you have a very round-shouldered art ... If
somehow I can, before I leave this earth, combine
my absolutely mad freedom and excitement with
truth, then I will have done something.*
— Andrew Wyeth

The Associated Press termed the psychological profile "eerily accurate." I felt the need to organize my thoughts about Dodd and the children. The investigation — the police work — underscored the truths of my psychiatric studies. My moral underpinnings were challenged and I had reached the limit. Art Curtis charged Dodd with three counts of aggravated first degree murder in connection with the deaths of three boys, and made it clear to the news media and anyone present that he would seek the death penalty. He expected two different trials. In the meantime, the court released my credentials, the affidavit for search warrant, and the profile. I was swamped under a media blitz of multiple press conferences, news programs and newspaper interviews. The media revealed the gruesome details of the murders and conversation about Dodd was inescapable. Everywhere I went, people were talking about the case. One night I was sitting in the bar at Opus II, and people seemed to be staring at me during a news break. Any excitement associated with celebrity status wore off quickly. I lost my privacy. People were even asking me about the humanity or inhumanity of the death penalty. I am not an expert on this subject and refused to discuss it even during television interviews. Pretrial hearings inflamed the public. Dodd's attorneys attempted to withhold his diary from the jury. Dodd, in the meantime, became a celebrity on network television talk shows. He even gave advice to parents and tried to advise the fathers of the three children he had killed. The media turns serial killers into celebrities as TV ratings go up and newspapers sell. In reality, these "cardboard people" are barren of accomplishment and devoid of any socially redeeming value, love or attachment. They are obviously not role models. I thought about the photo albums with clear evidence of post mortem sexual assault of little Lee. Dodd's attorneys now made motions to suppress the photographs lest they "incite" the jurors. I had to cooperate with Dodd's attorneys and investigators as they attempted to discredit my conclusions and the profile. They began an investigation of my personal life. I recall talking to one of Dodd's attorneys who laughed during our conversation. I thought he was worse than an animal. In preparation for my meeting with defense investigators, I reread sections of Dodd's diary.

11-4-89 - 11:10 P.M. Victim #3 will die by suffocation — plastic bag over his head. Bag will be secured after I suck him erect. As he suffocates to death (tied down of course) I'll keep sucking to keep him erect. Thanks to Lee I know I can't make a dead one erect, but will they stay erect if erect at the time of death?

11-10-89 - 10:20 P.M. - Instead of the bag, I'll tape his mouth shut, then, when ready, I'll use a clothespin or something to plug his nose. This way I can clearly see his face as he dies, as well as get some pictures of a naked, dying boy. This suffocation also eliminates the neck-rope burns, as Lee had in incident #2. Electrocution is also a good means for a quick death.

11-11-89 -7:30 P.M. to 10:00 P.M. At the movie *The Bear* (as in incident #2) to find a lone boy in bathroom. Talked to a 7-8 year old, who was not as cute in the lighted bathroom as he looked in the dark. He insisted no, I said "Okay. — wait here — I'll leave," then "No - you're coming with me" (changed my mind). I finally decided I couldn't.

Excerpt from Dodd's diary dealing with the suffocation scenario:

That way I can sit back, take pictures and watch him die, instead of concentrating on my hands or the rope tight around his neck — that would also eliminate the rope burns.

I knew that some serial killers tape record the screams of their tortured dying victims. This is for later replay and masturbatory fantasy activity. After reading the diary again, my blood was boiling. I was ready for Dodd's investigator — ready to fight! As it turned out, the defense's investigator came to my office. He was a real bozo — sloppy looking and dirty. He spent most of the time trying to convince me that Dodd hadn't killed anyone other than the three children, as if that were okay. This man was obviously hired with one purpose in mind and I found him to be a pushover without significance. By this time I knew that Dodd had molested more than 80 children and had been in the Washington and Idaho court systems over and over again. Yet he had served less than six months total time in jail. I was loaded for bear!

William Faulkner once wrote that if he had to choose between pain and nothing he would choose pain. I understood this, but as progress was being made in my analysis, I started to look for pleasure. I had learned a great deal about my past reluctance to be completely successful as it related to the guilt associated with my father's death. No longer did I feel I had to do more or be more. The most important thing that an analysis does is allow a person to be himself and to be *content* with himself. I wanted to spend time with friends, some of whom were women who had known both Joanne and me.

The healthy part of my ego was manifesting itself. In retrospect, I know I was looking for a Joanne substitute. I was haunted by the intense memory of passion we shared together.

One night, I met Joanne at a mid-week cocktail party, which was a fund-raiser for a children's residential treatment center. She tried to avoid me at first but we did talk. She said my colleagues were talking about me and described what she thought was an ostentatious display of pseudo-happiness and pulchritude. So much for my passing "girlfriends!" I was embarrassed. One of my colleagues also said he thought I was making a fool of myself. I really didn't think so. When I talked to Dave Bishop about some of these issues, his advice was like that of a Zen master. He simply told me to be more loving, more kind and more caring. He reminded me of help I had given him in the past in the confused world of police emotions.

I'm not sure whose idea it was but my former military friend, Igor, and I decided to meet in New York City. There was a psychiatry meeting we could at least pay token homage to. I arrived at the hotel, where we were sharing a room, before him and took a shower. As I was toweling off, Igor burst into the room wearing a huge leather jacket, threw his arms around me and yelled: "I've always wanted to hug a naked psychiatrist!" The door was still open and there were some people in the hall.

The following morning, he wanted to do a helicopter tour of the city to relive old times from the military. On the drive to the airport, we could see smoke from a nearby building blowing out of the stack at a ninety degree angle. I backed out at the last minute, but Igor had already gone in and purchased expensive tickets. The flight around the Statue of Liberty, Ellis Island and through Manhattan was wonderful and I'll be forever grateful we did it. I was truly enthralled and for at least an hour forgot my problems. We were cold when we landed and so went to *Petrouchka,* a Russian–French restaurant with Gypsy music in the basement. This was up at East 86th street. We consumed loads of caviar and more vodka than I want to think about. The bill, just for drinks and caviar, was over $400, Igor gave the waiter his sperm card — one could make deposits with it, but this did not go over. I paid the bill and stumbled out, still hungry. The next few days were a blur. We were evicted from one or two places because Igor would not wear a dinner jacket, and we left one establishment when a fist fight broke out. I had had enough fighting. It was wonderful being with such a trusted friend because I knew I could say and do anything without offending him. Even if some of our escapades were juvenile and foolish, the feeling was mutual. Igor also really knew New York and getting around was a cinch.

When I finally poured myself onto the plane back to Portland, I wondered why I couldn't always live this way. I believe I understood my relationship with Igor better. The intimacy was important — and no demands. He also freed me up to let loose to be myself and not take things too seriously. He also acted out behaviors that I was too shy or controlled to engage in and now I had been drawn into this previously vicarious lifestyle. There were likely elements of a father figure here with all of the love and acceptance implicit and explicit in such a relationship. I left New York feeling strengthened. Not only was my identity reaffirmed but I felt "new." I forgave myself the foolishness as part of the path back to normality.

I felt so new that the creative process or the crazy process took hold. For reasons that are still not completely clear to me, I decided to run off to Italy. That's how I thought of it. I guess I was getting in touch with my "authentic" self — in many respects my old spontaneous self. Joanne and I had run off to Greece one year on the spur of the moment and another time, while sitting in a restaurant, we decided to leave for Portugal. That time we ended up in the revolution.

So, off to Italy it would be. I had blown some negatives out of proportion — gotten into some filth — and maybe things would change. Oh, this wasn't what was in my conscious mind, but I'm sure it was there. After all, this mess with Dodd had exacted a heavy price — my marriage. Going to Rome was a big deal in Freud's life. He had waited until he was highly successful before making the trip and, once there, developed vertigo and became highly disoriented — a product of his neurosis. He later resolved the unconscious derivatives of his neurosis in his own analysis. Most important for me, however, was the issue of my own roots. I have always loved and felt at home in Italy. Arriving in Rome mid-morning, I took a taxi to the hotel. The streets were packed with people and, near the hotel, I asked the taxi driver, a taciturn fellow for an Italian, to let me out. Walking towards the hotel near the Spanish Steps, I spotted an Italian soldier with his bivouac cap pushed back on his head in a carefree manner. He was eating a strawberry ice cream cone and it was as if he was putting his entire life into it. I thought of all the young kid-soldiers I had known and of my brothers. With a mixture of bittersweet joy and delight, I burst out laughing. The soldier caught my expression, grinned and saluted me with his ice-cream cone! His grin defined the day — and my new life. I was finding myself. Go to Rome and find yourself, I thought. Silly.... I laughed all the way to the hotel. This was Italy! The Italy of warmth and animation. The Italians and their more reserved cousins, the Spanish, stand in stark contrast to the pushy and arrogant German tourists one finds in Latin countries during vacation time. It's as if the Germans go to Southern Europe to get a dose of humanity but it doesn't stick. One of my German doctor colleagues told me how dismayed the Germans were during World War II as Italian families flocked to the train stations, hugging and kissing their sons, and crying as they went off to war. In the meantime, the Germans were killing innocent Norwegian and British prisoners.

Settling into Rome, I had lunch at a different cafe every day and made no specific plans. One afternoon while drinking my second glass of wine, something I would never do in the States, I noticed a woman a few tables away. The short skirt and bronzed legs caught my attention first. Then I noticed her sensual, yet sharp, features, her sundress pouring across her body in the gentle breeze. Sunglasses perched in her reddish-brown hair. She wore open-toed shoes and no stockings. A bracelet on her left wrist, a small wristwatch and no wedding ring.

Her olive skin was stunning. Her deep, dark brown eyes caught me off balance. All in a moment, I fantasized getting to my feet — maybe it was the wine that did it — walking to her table and introducing myself. In that instant, I saw all the things that could happen between us. I saw myself telling her about my roommate in college who studied architecture. He lived in Enfield, Connecticut. Did she know him? We would talk and talk and talk. Mostly she would talk. I saw myself listening, mesmerized by her smile, deep brown eyes and sensuous movements. Her touch brought tears to my eyes and I could barely believe the sensations in my skin. She was traveling with friends, and she would invite me to join them for dinner that evening, and I would be readily accepted into the group. My fantasy! And I knew when she smiled invitingly back at me from across her table that it could all be true, if I took that first step.

I didn't, of course, not because of restraint, but because her freshness, her ripe loveliness made me think of sweet, enchanting moments with Joanne. She made me realize how much I missed my wife.

When I returned to my hotel, I threw the French windows open and a fragrant breeze came through, bathing me with delight, a sensuous messenger that gave me visions of romance and a touch of whimsical regret for the sun-tanned, golden woman who made me think of Joanne.

I didn't know what I had to do. A long way from Portland, I was cut out of time. I had no country, no friends, no patients, no parents — no other life. Nothing existed but the moment, my memories of Joanne mixed-up with the dark-eyed, inviting stranger and Italy.

The following morning my stay in Italy came to an end. I knew I was still confused about my life. Was there still hope with Joanne? Did I even want to stay married at this point? During the flight from Nice to Paris, I recalled Lincoln's comments: "I am now the most miserable man living. If what I feel were equally distributed to the whole human family, there would not be one cheerful face on earth." All the losses of my life were coming out. But I knew that if Joanne and I were to be reunited, I would have to come back to her as a whole human being.

Chapter 15

Does God Throw Dice?

It is only to the individual that a soul is given.
– Albert Einstein

In 1949, Richard Feynman established the mathematical formulations of particle interactions in quantum theory with space-time diagrams. This was the result of modern physics and a radical notion of the universe. Quantum theory implies that we cannot decompose the world into independently small units, paving the way for a union of life force and wave-particle reality. Quantum theory and relativity theory have made it clear that reality transcends classical logic. Heisenberg, Bohr, Planck, Einstein and a host of other physicists laid the groundwork for an understanding of probability concepts in the universe and the concept of uncertainty — in a certain sense the law of causality becomes invalid. The association of an effect and the temporal sequence of cause and effect undermined classical ways of thinking about the physical universe. Once again, man discovered that the universe was not what he thought it was, precise and measurable but open to variation and chance.

Although Einstein paved the way for these theories as early as 1920, he expressed opposition to quantum theory and told Bohr: "God does not play dice." Heisenberg himself supported efforts to link contemporary physics to Taoist philosophy and Eastern religion. Contemporary theologians are working on a kind of unified field theory of religion by exploring the similarities of all religions and their intrinsic meaning and universal value, not irrespective of mysticism. Theoretical physics does and will play a major role in man's understanding of God and the relevance of religion in our daily lives. "Science without religion is blind, and religion without science is lame," said Einstein. The application of scientific principles to spiritual under-standing eliminates the compartmentalization of science and religion.

The psychoanalyst, however, studies the reality behind religion, leading to contemplation of the age old question of whether God plays a role in our daily lives, specifically on an individual level. For some, the answer is easy. For Ghandi, God appeared not in person but in action. This also means that man cannot be comprehended in isolation from his creative social action. Who casts our role and why? Who are the dancers, and who the dance? It was interesting to me, as a mental note, that the Dodd case could in some convoluted fashion be related to great ideas. But then, even violent death is part of life, I thought.

My return to Portland was uneventful. Marcia Coffey, a reporter for KOIN-TV, spoke to Dodd during a recess in jury selection and reported differences his attorneys were having as to whether he should testify in his own defense.

Clark County Superior Court Judge Robert Harris ordered
his deputies to keep Dodd from talking to anyone other than
his lawyers. He considered issuing a gag order. Westley
Allan Dodd had always wanted to plead guilty, but his
defense attorneys repeatedly talked him out of this. Finally,
on June 11, 1990, he stood before Judge Robert Harris and
said he wanted to change his plea from innocent to guilty.
He openly confessed to his crimes and admitted premeditation. Before this time, on May 8, I appeared in court for
what is known as a suppression hearing and testified
regarding the video interview we made of Dodd on
November 15. Then video was allowed, admissible. The
defense tried to discredit the profile and suppress the video,
but I said I acted, not as a physician, but as a police officer.
Roger Bennett, the Clark County chief deputy prosecutor,
was to bring the case before a jury of six men and six
women. Dodd's diary was used along with other evidence.
Dodd had used such phrases as "the hunt" or "a good place
for rape and murder or kidnap, rape and murder … a good
hunting ground." Art Curtis spoke to the jury about the
enormity of the crimes. Washington's penalty trials never
end in a mistrial because of a hung jury. A jury's unanimous
finding in favor of the prosecution's argument returns a
verdict of death by lethal injection or hanging. If there is a
split among the jury, the verdict is life in the state peniten-
tiary without possibility of parole. In Washington, only a
governor's pardon can alter such a sentence. In other states,
a judge can alter a life sentence. Under an agreement with
the prosecuting attorneys in the Dodd case, the charges
against him were consolidated into a single trial to be heard
by a single jury. Prosecutors could present evidence not
ordinarily heard during a trial. Dodd's attorneys attempted
to withhold evidence from the jury and the public was

incensed. The defense attorneys did not want the jury to hate Dodd. Roger Bennett argued that defense motions to suppress evidence amounted to an effort to "desensitize the entire incident — to sanitize it.... This isn't evidence the state has manufactured," he said, "It is the direct product of the defendant's actions. We offer photographs of Mr. Dodd's handiwork — what he created or what he destroyed by his acts." The jury of six men and six women heard that Dodd kept Polaroid photos of his rape and strangulation of Lee Iseli and that he had made a pact with Satan seeking assistance in finding and killing his future victims.

Dodd's devastating quote affirming his prayer to the Devil and an excerpt from his diary made clear the alliance he sought with the Prince of Darkness:

> Over the past few months I have been asking in various ways for Satan to assist me in my quest....
>
> I just had a dream ... I was on what must have been an ocean beach. There was a swirl in the sand and a dried-out starfish was sucked under the surface of the sand. Then either a new swirl or maybe a continuation of the first one sucked up some sort of plant. The swirl grew a little larger, forming a sinkhole in the center. Using a small army-type shovel I began digging out the center of the swirl. I quickly broke through into an underground hole of some sort, and made the opening a little bigger, though I was sure it didn't need much help. Then a person I recognized as Satan poked his head up through the hole in the sand.... As a result of my dream or meeting, I believe in Satan and am prepared to enter into a contract with him.

The legal delays, continuances and maneuverings had served no purpose — jurors were told that Dodd had designed a torture rack on which he intended to perform "experimental surgery" on young children, mutilating their sexual organs while they were still alive. At one point, one juror in his mid-thirties nearly passed out and the judge called a recess.

I had appeared on a television program prior to the trial and was relieved that there would be no defense of mental disease or defect. Actually, the defense made no opening statement and produced no witnesses in Dodd's defense. Dodd remained impassive during the trial. When I testified at the suppression hearing, he did not look at me. In an interview with the *Oregonian* he said he was bored by the testimony. "I've heard it all so many times now. It's kind of old, really." As far as I was concerned, Dodd was as good as dead. I found Psalm 109:7: "When he shall be judged, let him be condemned: and let his prayer become sin." The profile, the investigation, the suppression hearing and now the trial. Little chance that a jury would vote for leniency, but you never know. They might, like my police friend, think he was crazy. After deliberating 14 hours over three days, on Saturday, July 14, 1990, jurors reached a unanimous verdict in favor of the death penalty. Judge Harris had instructed the jury that mental competency was never an issue in the case and so that was that! I'm sure that was a tough weekend for all the jurors.

The reactions were idiosyncratic. Dodd's reaction to the verdict was in stark contrast to that of the jurors. Juror Jeffrey McEllrath had recurring nightmares, not unlike my own, since the trial began. We were part of the same human family. Had McEllrath known the magnitude of the case at its outset, he would have excused himself from jury duty, or at least tried. Lyle Bame, the jury's foreman, said: "I don't think it'll ever be over. It'll be within us forever. Every time

I see a tennis shoe or a bicycle it just makes me shiver."

The victims' parents were relieved. The monster would be punished. Robert Iseli and Clair Neer embraced each other. Ray Graves, the man who stopped the kidnapping of James Kirk from the Liberty Theater, joined in. Said Neer, "At last, something went my way. Finally, they got that piece of garbage off the street." Iseli, not an advocate of the death penalty, said, "One thing we have to remember is that we are not killing Westley Dodd. We're killing someone else. Many years ago Westley Allan died. Someday, hopefully, there will be a time when we won't have to hear his name again." Echoes of Jane Simons' concept of soul death. I understood Iseli's concept, because a number of my patients died after lingering illnesses, a shadow of their former existence and different people. Outside the courtroom, Ray Graves said: "The man don't deserve to live — not someone who does that to babies. There's nothing more precious than them little guys."

Markedly absent from the proceedings was Dodd's family. His father and stepmother had visited him in jail shortly after his arrest, but his father felt guilty about what had happened and didn't want to see him again. Dodd's younger brother was away, serving in the navy, and his natural mother simply cried when Dodd's name was mentioned. His sister made no comment to the media. She would not talk.

At the formal sentence hearing on July 26, Judge Harris signed the formal death sentence. Dodd was also given a 50-year prison term for the attempted murder of James Kirk. This was three times the number of years recommended under Washington's sentencing guidelines. No one was taking any chances. Harris said the term was warranted given the age of Dodd's intended victim and the nature of his sadistic crimes. If the death penalty were struck down or repealed in Washington, Dodd could be eligible for release. Judge Harris wanted to make sure that didn't happen. He said: "Dodd has an ongoing, depraved, sadistic desire to hurt, injure and maim others, and murder is the ultimate goal, the ultimate satisfaction." He had defined the malignant-narcissistic personality.

Dodd's case would now be up for appeal. The national average for appeals on death penalty cases is ten years, but Dodd's decision to plead guilty eliminated many of the issues that could be appealed. He, himself, said he expected the death sentence and indeed wanted it. He did not plan to appeal. He, in opposition to his attorneys, wanted to "streamline his trip to the gallows" and objected to any appeal on his behalf. He also wanted to hang because that is how he killed Lee Iseli. He had previously confided this thought to me long before the trial. Dodd was placed at the Walla Walla prison, where he conducted interviews and television appearances. As is common with serial killers, he achieved some degree of celebrity status. While Jensen, Trimble, Buckner and I were dodging the press and keeping a low profile, Dodd almost needed an agent to program his appearances. He gave extensive media interviews from jail and even advice to parents on teaching their children to avoid child molesters. Some thought they could learn from him and the rest of us snickered. Many were outraged at Dodd's suggestion that somehow the public was responsible for his actions because they had failed to stop him, a theme he confided to me as well. Karen Osborne was appointed as spokeswoman for the Iseli family and noted: "The final evil deeds are Dodd's alone."

That summer, I prepared to be in the bridal party of a fellow police officer. It was very hot, but the wedding was a distraction full of love as it was. I made no note of Dodd's sentencing in my calendar and started to distance everything — the name, the words, the people — everything. Fishing was lousy that summer, or was it me? Had I lost my touch? My sense of unease continued. The Washington Supreme Court had a hearing on the case and there were attempts to prevent Dodd's hanging. The American Civil Liberties Union filed a lawsuit in Olympia protesting the hanging as cruel and unusual punishment.

Several months before Westley Allan Dodd even committed his crimes, another sex offender, Earl Kenneth Shriner, was up for trial in Bellingham, Washington. The charges included raping, choking and mutilating an eight-year-old boy. This man had a 24-year history of molestation and sexual crimes. The Northwest population was shocked and Shriner was convicted. The Washington legislature passed a series of statutes in 1990 that related to the registration of sexual offenders, including longer sentences.

On January 25, 1990, Dodd mailed a letter to Governor Booth Gardner agreeing with the statutes that had been passed. He noted: "I mean for this letter to be used to help stop others like myself. Also, do not forget about the juvenile offenders. I started when I was 13 or 14 years old. By the time I graduated from high school, I had been caught five times, and reported to the police only three times." Dodd prepared a booklet of instruction to parents and teachers. He appeared on national television including the *Donahue* program and later on *Sally Jessy Raphael.* He "interviewed" the victim's parents and engaged in ongoing dialogue. Although I shunned the media, I did agree to appear on the CBS program *48 Hours,* hosted by Dan Rather. My appearance was prompted by strong encouragement from the law enforcement community to represent the police and tell the true story. Dodd was also interviewed for the program. The CBS team that went to the Walla Walla prison to videotape him for the program told me they thought he was getting vicarious sexual pleasure from the experience.

Around this time, I took a trip to Santa Fe and sat in a sweat lodge. I thought about producing a book of photographs of Native American children. I also considered a vision quest. During this time, I went over to the Navajo reservation in Arizona and visited with an ancient Navajo woman who lived in a hogan. Her furniture, including a large quilted bed, was in the middle of the earthen dirt floor of her home. She gave me a small bracelet and out in the sunshine I studied the lines in her face. "Grandmother" — a word of respect for Navajos. The flight back to Portland was quick and smooth.

On January 4, 1993, Westley Allan Dodd was hanged. I had been asked to participate in a television panel previous to, during and following the hanging. I refused. I did not watch the televised event nor did I follow the news accounts. Later, we learned that Dodd's neck did not break as the hangman had planned, but he strangled to death. Just like Lee Iseli.

It did not escape my conscious memory that January was the month of my father's death.

The screws on the casket began to dissolve before my very eyes. My God! Dodd's body had become moldy and began to move in a turning screw-like fashion as the casket deteriorated further. I watched in disbelief — another horror heaped upon horrors! How could this be? Dodd had only been dead a short time. I thought of medical school — the cadavers. Freshman anatomy — but that had a purpose — it was rational. As I stared, the casket crumbled. I had turned to run but couldn't move fast enough. Soaked in perspiration and moaning — like a Munch painting — scream. I thought of the Navy Seals I had known. They could get out of the most impossible situations. I had measured myself against these men — real men, honorable men. Moving a little was an almost impossible struggle. With my back to the casket, I jerked forward.

Bolt upright in bed and soaked in perspiration, I glanced at the digital clock — 3:20 A.M. What was real? What was dream? The Australian aborigines have their dream time — another reality while we sleep. My "dream time" was haunted. I left the room and wrote the dream down. More work for analysis. I was, however painfully, getting there.

In response to Einstein's comment that God does not throw dice, Niels Bohr replied, "Nor is it our business to prescribe to God how He should run the world."

Chapter 12

A Summer's Day

Shall I compare thee to a summer's day?
Thou art more lovely and more temperate:
Rough winds do shake the darling buds of May,
And summer's lease hath all too short a date:
Sometime too hot the eye of heaven shines,
And often is his gold complexion dimm'd;
And every fair from fair sometime declines,
By chance, or nature's changing course
*   untrimm'd;*
But thy eternal summer shall not fade,
Nor lose possession of that fair thou ow'st,
Nor shall death brag thou wander'st in his
*   shade,*
When in eternal lines to time thou grow'st:
So long as men can breathe, or eyes can see,
So long lives this, and this gives life to thee.
*   – William Shakespeare*

It was the best and worst of times. A time of rest and a time of forgiveness. A season of journeys. It was Einstein who said that "whoever cannot contemplate or know the deep shudder of the soul to enchantment, might as well be dead, for he has already closed his eyes upon life."

When I was a medical student at The Jefferson Medical College in Philadelphia, one of my classmates, a fine fellow, never seemed to do well in his classes. With everyone's help, he managed to make it to his third year — the clinical year. We rotated through various surgical and medical specialties to learn, practice and perhaps sample our future. When this young man came upon a surgical subspecialty, he came to life and became an A student. I watched and understood this, having had a similar experience in high school. In adolescence, my desire was to attend Central High School — a public institution that opened its doors to the most promising and intelligent students in the community. It was a special school with a rigorous academic program and an endowment. My brother, much more intelligent than I, had broken precedent and gone there. Somehow, I passed the entrance examinations and thanks to a Dr. Cornog, the headmaster, I matriculated — two weeks late. Several eye surgeries delayed school entrance that year. The first semester, I failed all subjects. The second was a little better with three failures out of five. Determined, I took a summer job and went to summer school. I studied while eating meals on the public transportation system. Most of the professors were encouraging but I had trouble with the English language, having grown up in a household where Italian was the primary language. I knew little of singular, plural, syntax or case. The public schools had simply passed me along, a common scenario these days also.

By the second year at Central, I managed C's and D's. My German professor taught me grammar while my English professor ridiculed me before the all male student body. He was an "English Gentleman." By my third year I made the Barnwell Honor Roll in spite of continued barely passing marks in English. Senior English was a stumbling block for most students because of the great emphasis put on the study of Shakespeare. Quite a few students failed and could not graduate or had to take the year over. Things were not looking good for me — a marginal English student at best. As luck would have it, I pulled the most difficult teacher in the school for my classes — Bertram Barsky. I prepared to fail the senior year and was not sure I could afford to take another year at this prestigious school.

Our first play was *Romeo and Juliet.* Unbelievably, I fell in love with the play, the language and Shakespeare. Dr. Barsky changed my life forever. That year he took me to the theater to see — of all things — *Romeo and Juliet.* There is a warm spot that will be forever in my heart for this wonderful man who opened up the English language and Shakespearean literature to me.

Ashland is a town in southern Oregon not far from the California border. Much can be written about this enchanting place. In 1935, Angus L. Bowmer founded the Oregon Shakespearean Festival, representing the finest professional Shakespearean production anyplace in the world. There are three theaters, the outdoor Elizabethan Stage, the ultra-modern Angus Bowmer Theater and the Black Swan. The first two theaters present Shakespeare and the Black Swan offers more contemporary plays such as those of Ibsen or Durang. The entire community *is* Shakespeare and it's not unusual to meet the actors and actresses off stage. The town motto is, "Where there is a Will there is a play." Practically every business establishment has a Shakespearean motto and the streets are decorated in Elizabethan decor. There are backstage tours where you can play with the props or take photographs. There are Elizabethan inns for dining and a host of activities related to the plays. Joanne and I love Shakespeare — not as entertainment, but as life. For us, Shakespeare lives. Shakespeare lives in Ashland. For twenty years we have made the pilgrimage, mostly during summer months, to the plays.

It was natural that my instincts would fall back onto something as basic as Will Shakespeare. I love Dickens — not Joanne's forte — and many of the British "old school." When the dream came I don't know how but it set into motion a series of happenings that was to culminate in a dramatic turn of events. I would never have foreseen the changes that would occur.

"Look Joanne — there's a beautiful cat on our window sill. A tomcat with golden stripes. The sun is shining on it." That was it. My first association to this dream was to the tabby tomcat that Goombah had. Goombah is an affectionate Italian name for trusted friend or beneficent "uncle." Someone you can love and trust. Goombah was the carpenter who lived across the street from my boyhood home. He smelled of cigars and wine, and sometimes invited me to visit him. Much to the consternation of his wife who yelled in the background, he gave me cigars, wine and nuts and treated me like a man. "Mrs. Goombah" worried about what my mother might say if she found out or if I might get sick from the tobacco and alcohol. Although I left feeling dizzy, I never did get sick and kept the secret to myself. I gloried in my sense of male community, of being grown up, capable of handling

things. The next association involved my knowledge of Egyptian history and the elevation of cats in that culture. Cats protected the vast grain food supplies from destruction by rats and were elevated to the status of gods. This led to the issues of good versus evil and finally to my association of the last scene in the movie *Blue Velvet*. All of this from a cat on a window sill! That's how analysis works! After this dream, I knew I was ready for something, but I didn't know what. The dream ultimately pointed to police related issues. Tom was my closest boyhood friend and his father was the police detective. *Blue Velvet* deals with the triumph of good over evil by innocence with the help of the police.

My work at least was going along reasonably well, the office was orderly and I began writing again. I agreed to present a paper in New York and started studying. My social life took a back seat partly because I felt awkward in new situations but mostly because I felt lost. Things were coming back together though. Joanne continued to leave notes on my desk when she had a question about some office procedure or when I had to follow up with a public appearance or respond to a request to give a talk. Our heating unit broke down and, by exchanging notes, we decided to purchase a new one. It was expensive, but Joanne handled the details and brought the service people in, saving me valuable time that I could donate to my profession. I heard that she was moving up in her work and was appointed to the Citizens Review Board, a panel reviewing, studying and hearing cases of child abuse. I also heard that she was the one everyone wanted to chair one of the panels. Naturally, my curiosity never ended.

I guess it was an impulse. Is anything ever an accident? A coincidence? What role did this dream play?

Of my trip to Italy, trying to define its meaning to me, I finally concluded that the country's soft ambience and storied loveliness offered exile for loneliness. It was a compatible land and welcomed those groping for a smile, the touch of a hand, a warm heart that cherishes. But oh, that poor wretched, seared and blackened soul, the hanged man, whose own terrible exile led him to blot out the light in his victim's eyes.

I decided to leave a Shakespearean sonnet on Joanne's desk at home. "Shall I compare thee to a summer's day?" My special book on the sonnets was in the office and I wrote it out by hand and left it before going off to work. Our relationship had settled into pleasant and reasonable encounters, yet they were distant.

I went home early that afternoon to see if she had found it and to check the response. I was hopeful, anxious and impatient. Actually, I cancelled all my patients from noon on and couldn't wait any longer. The garage door opened and I noticed her Cherokee still parked inside. My chest muscles were tight and I was breathless as I jumped the first three steps and opened the door to the hall. I ran down the corridor leading to our desks and noticed that the note with the sonnet had been moved. She read it but left it on the desk. Probably thought it was a stupid ploy, I thought. I turned aside to look at the mail on my desk and saw it. A note.

"Ron, how about dinner? The Heathman at 7."

The Heathman is a bar–restaurant in Portland, an upscale kind of place — sophisticated and classy. Joanne and I used to reserve it for special occasions like birthdays and anniversaries. I immediately, instinctively, sensed the significance of her note and my eyes filled with tears. Joanne, coming down from the upper levels entered the room as I was holding the note. I looked up at this beautiful, warm, wonderful, sensuous, tall woman dressed in jeans and a Western-style plaid shirt. This sophisticated person — this lovable body before me. *Where had I been?* Our touch and embrace was magical beyond belief. For a few moments I couldn't talk.

Joanne broke the silence: "Ron, it's nice to have you home."

To order additional copies of

Closely Watched Shadows

Book: $14.95   Shipping/Handling $3.50

Call *BookPartners, Inc.*
1-800-895-7323